The GREAT LIFE Handbook

Published by Spines
ISBN: 979-8-89569-883-9

The GREAT LIFE Handbook

Building a Healthy Relationship with Love, Fear, Purpose, and Death

LESTER F. STRONG

Contents

Dedication

Eckhart Tolle
Your book Stillness Speaks has inspired this one.
Thank you.

Patrice
On a narrow, winding Dingle road overlooking Blasket Island,
we conceived this book.
Thank you.

Leela, Kelli, Alex, Rachel and Neil
"Where you are now, I once was. Where I am, you shall be.
Prepare yourself to follow me."
(New England gravestone)
I love you.

Acknowledgments

To Evry Mann, Therese Bimka, Susan Richmann, Jeanne McGough, Mark Houghtaling, and Rik Flynn, who are the true editors of this book. Our many years of painstakingly distilling sacred/secular topics is the crucible in which this book has been forged.
Thank you.

To members of the Sunday Gathering, you have been a reliable testing ground for many of the case studies contained in this book.
Thank you.

About the Author

LESTER STRONG has studied and practiced Yoga and meditation for over forty years across North America, Europe, Australia, and India. He held multiple positions in television as a journalist, producer, and executive producer over a twenty-five-year career in Charlotte, Atlanta, New York City, and Boston. Lester has received numerous awards for his broadcasting work, including a White House commendation and five regional EMMY awards. Lester lives in Florida with his wife, Patrice Courtney-Strong.

A Little More About Lester

My earliest memories as a child are just flashes of images, people, and feelings in no coherent or logical pattern. We lived in the Negro section (this was the 50s) of a public housing project in Whitaker, Pennsylvania, just outside of Pittsburgh, overlooking the Monongahela River. Across the river in Braddock, where I would spend most of my childhood and adolescence, was the Edgar Thompson Steel Mill, one of the largest in the country at the time. It was a magnet for workers from multiple ethnicities: Black Americans born in the Pittsburgh area and those who migrated up from the South, many first- and second-generation Americans with Eastern and Western European ancestry, Chinese-Americans, Catholics, Jews, Protestants, and Pentecostals. They were all determined to find a decent job that would feed and house their families.

Forty-five B Midway Drive in Whitaker was a row house with a first and second floor and a coal furnace. I know that because I remember the coal bin in the back of our unit. I remember having a sense of boundless exuberance and curiosity. As a small child, one of my favorite games was trying to leap from one street curb to the next like Superman. I remember thinking, "This time I'll do it." While I did play with other children, my two closest friends between ages three and six were imaginary, and I would have conversations with Jesus or God. I definitely conflated the two. Somewhere between ages six and nine, my sense of possibility and imagination shifted into intense rage and mistrust. In many ways, this book is about the return to that joyful, imaginative, and curious little boy.

I can't leave this section without acknowledging both my parents' and my siblings' impact on my life. It's impossible not to have been touched by the people I lived with intimately for 19 years and have known for more than 75 years. My childhood and adolescent years were a very difficult time for me. But maturity and grace have allowed me to better appreciate the harsh challenges that both my parents and siblings endured as well.

Dennis and Mozelle Strong, my parents, grew up in Jim Crow North Carolina until they migrated to Pittsburgh during World War II. My mother was the youngest of 14 children and the only one in her family to attend and graduate from college, the historically Black Winston-Salem State Teachers College. My father was one of three children and was educated through the eighth grade. That's all most Black students, especially males, could expect at that time in the rural South. He immediately went to work to help support his family.

Evidence of my mother's love for books was everywhere. For me, her most precious and enduring gift was a full set of the Encyclopedia Britannica, followed closely by subscriptions to *Jet* and *Ebony* magazines which, along with the *Pittsburgh*

Courier, were my only access to Black history and culture growing up.

The inescapable lesson from my father was simply how to slavishly endure hard work in order to provide for his family. He worked at least two, sometimes three, jobs in a given week, never earning more than $30,000 in his working life. Yet he was also entrepreneurial, creating his own dry-cleaning business which he ran for more than 50 years. It's still operating and remains in the family.

In some spiritual traditions, it's believed that we choose the families we're born into in order to learn vital lessons on this earthly plane. If that's true, one of those critical lessons for me this lifetime must have been to develop greater love and compassion for others. At a very young age, I felt no special bond to my parents nor my eight siblings growing up. As we became adults, I did cultivate closer relationships with some of my brothers and sisters more than others, but those connections were based more on who they were as persons rather than any shared family history. The lack of any emotional connection, first with my family and then with a variety of people and events, has been the persistent challenge throughout my life. My struggle to develop a consistent sense of closeness, trust, and commitment has been the primary impetus for much of my spiritual exploration. Thankfully, I think I have evolved from mutually beneficial transactions to cultivating truly unconditional giving and receiving relationships.

This is a spiritual book. How could it be otherwise? There are pivotal moments in my life that have brought me to this present view of myself, the world, and beyond. Without question, I now consider every aspect of my life grist for rich spiritual exploration.

It's important to define terms as we go through this book since some of the terms are subject to multiple definitions and interpretations. I'll start with what spirituality means to me: *the quest to fully understand the temporal and spiritual dimensions of my Self and to apply that understanding through selfless service and living harmoniously with people, the planet, and Universal Consciousness.*

In the science of living things, no plant or animal can survive in complete isolation. It must have air, water, sunlight, food, etc., to live. To fully understand what it means to be a human being, we first must develop an intimate understanding of how we function on both physical and metaphysical levels. Then we can forge a true connection with other people, Nature, and Universal Consciousness. Throughout this book, I will use the terms *Consciousness, Universal Consciousness, Universal Intelligence, and Natural Intelligence* interchangeably. They all speak to the one ultimate reality that permeates and animates everything in existence, both seen and unseen. Astrophysicist Neil deGrasse Tyson is fond of saying that we humans are made up of particles from distant stars and planets. Where and how exactly does humanity fit into this cosmic paradigm? The highest purpose of human existence is to answer that question.

Quantum physicists have determined that a single particle of mass/energy (Higgs boson or the god particle) is the smallest substance yet to be contained in all animate and inanimate substances in the cosmos, from the breath of every living thing to the planets orbiting one another. This phenomenon affirms that there is one common intelligence that links everything in existence. Einstein, through his Unified Field Theory, tried unsuccessfully to capture a formula for the existence of this universal energy/intelligence which drives all activity in the cosmos.

What scientists have worked so diligently to fully grasp, mystics, yogis, saints, and philosophers have known for millennia. These wise ones tell us that we can never completely comprehend Universal Consciousness through the thinking mind alone, but that we can experience it fully, because we *are* it—which is how we ultimately align with everything that exists.

I keep referring to scientific principles to highlight the convergence of scientific and spiritual findings about the Ultimate Reality even though their approaches may differ. Western thought is steeped in the firm conviction that through the thinking mind/intellect, human beings can perceive the highest level of Reality. However, a long line of spiritual teachers, mystics, poets, and philosophers assert that the thinking mind can only lead to a limited sensory and emotional experience of who we are. To be clear, cultivating what I'm calling the thinking mind is necessary, even vital, to evolve as a species. But also, I strongly suggest that love or joy or peace or insight/inspiration cannot be reduced to biology or physics. My firm conviction is grounded in limited but profound experiences of going beyond the mind/intellect.

I was lucky enough to spend quality time with Alex Haley over both beers and breakfast in the 70s. Alex was the author of *Roots* 1 and *The Autobiography of Malcolm X*. He once explained to me that tribes in the Gambia, where he traced his ancestry, had a ceremony (adapted for *The Lion King*) where they would hold newborns up to the stars and say, "Behold the only thing greater than yourself." However, the wise ones of many spiritual traditions would say to those same infants: *"Behold! You are greater than even this!"* They would say we humans are greater than the galaxies, greater even than the space that holds them. Lebanese poet Kahlil Gibran said it so beautifully in his epic poem, *The Prophet*: *"When you love you should not say 'God is in my heart,' but rather, 'I am in the heart of God.'"*

The goal of this book is to chart a pathway to a direct, continuous experience of that greatness... and to invite you onto the journey as well. This unbroken awareness, which is the essence of pure love, is where every human being ultimately belongs.

Foreword

Lester Strong has given us a wonderful gift with the publication of *The Great Life Handbook*. Running counter to the tenor of our times, this book is not a guide to getting rich or influencing people but rather a roadmap to a full and meaningful life. Based on his many years of study and practice, Lester focuses on the key elements of human existence: *love, fear, purpose, and death.*

Most importantly, he not only provides analysis of these elements but also practical steps for us to take to realize our full potential. Key to this are meditation and intention, and he offers resources and exercises that serve as guideposts and inspiration. This detailed grounding in the reality of our daily lives is what makes this book so special.

There are quotes and links herein that the reader can use as daily nourishment and return to as inspiration calls. This need not be a solitary practice; in fact, we are encouraged to work with this material within a small circle of friends. *Ubuntu 2* in application—we are all in this together.

As the author notes: "The goal of this book is to chart a pathway to a direct, continuous experience of that greatness… and to invite you onto the journey as well. This unbroken awareness, which is the essence of pure love, is where every human being ultimately belongs."

May this text be as great a blessing to you as it has proven to be for me.

Evry Mann, Founding member of the *Sunday Gathering*.

Introduction

There was something formless and perfect before the universe was born. It is serene. Empty. Solitary. Unchanging. Infinite. Eternally present. It is the Mother of the universe. For lack of a better name, I call it the Tao.... To know earth, understand heaven. To know heaven, understand the Way. To know the Way, understand the great within yourself.

— 25th Verse, Tao Te Ching

The 25th verse of the *Tao Te Ching* urges us to first deeply explore ourselves in order to understand (experience) the full dimension of Universal Intelligence—because we and the Tao, pure Consciousness, are really the same essence. By fully aligning ourselves with pure Consciousness and the principles that govern this limitless force (the Way), we connect with the same consciousness everywhere: in humanity, in nature, in the universe, and even in what existed before the physical universe was born.

In my early years as a Yoga student, there was an aphorism framed on a wall behind the teacher's chair. It read: "Only one who obeys can command." Almost 50 years later, I'm just beginning to glimpse the profound wisdom contained in that sutra. Like so many wisdom teachings, true insight comes only through deep contemplation and lived experience. To obey is to surrender our ego-centered intelligence and will to our Universal Intelligence and Will. Then our actions are no longer driven by either desire or fear of the outcome but are instead lovingly commanded by the divine principles of unconditional love and respect for everyone impacted by those actions, including ourselves. In the same way, airplanes command the skies only by obeying the laws of aerodynamics. And the Bible declares, "Not my will but Thy will be done" (Luke 22:42).

The title of this book is *The Great Life Handbook: Building a Healthy Relationship with Love, Fear, Purpose, and Death* because, as the *Tao Te Ching* explains, every human being has the capacity to experience a vastly greater reality than the sensory-driven reality that consumes most of us. It's an invitation to live from the space of supreme love and compassion for ourselves and for the world.

This book offers what I hope are practical approaches to the practice of self-exploration. I hope it's a book you'll come back to again and again as a reference guide for navigating both the joys and challenges of your life.

The simple premise of this book is to develop a healthy relationship with four unavoidable dimensions of life with which every human being will engage, either consciously or unconsciously. They are Love, Fear, Purpose, and Death. By using the indispensable contemplative tools of Meditation and Intention, we can develop a conscious and life-affirming relationship with each of these dimensions, and our life becomes great. The goal is not about achieving wealth, prestige, or power, although they are often the byproducts of a life lived with integrity. The goal is the journey itself. This book is about striving to be your Best Self in every moment of your life... starting right now.

And finally, I encourage you to read this book with a small group of friends, family, neighbors, and colleagues. Three to six people is the optimal size. What this book requires is vigilance and a commitment to practice its principles. For that, it's best to be part of a mutually supportive team. In Part I, it is invaluable to hear different perspectives on Meditation and Intention and to understand how your fellow explorers are wrestling with their intentions for Love, Fear, Purpose, and Death.

In Part II, you'll be asked to apply your intentions to a series of topical essays, which will be all the more enriched by other voices and insights. Once you've finished examining the essays in this book, I hope you will create a *Best Self Circle* (nothing sacred about the name), which continues to explore topics from the news, television, movies, books, social media, or simply from moments in everyday life as a way to enhance and accelerate your spiritual growth. I've been blessed to be part of such a group, called the Sunday Gathering, for many years.

At the end of the book are two appendices that I think you will find very valuable. In Appendix A, you'll find quotes from well known figures about love, fear, purpose and death. In Appendix B, you will find hyperlinks to videos, key terms, and definitions found throughout the book. This will be particularly helpful for readers of the printed version of the book.

As a young television reporter, I had the good fortune to meet and interview Archbishop Desmond Tutu, who helped to revive the indigenous South African philosophy of Ubuntu: "I am because you are." At its core, Ubuntu is about interdependent relationships—both humans to humans and humans to Nature. We human beings are hardwired for social interaction. It's how we learn. To the extent that humans and Nature thrive, we all thrive. To the extent that human beings and Nature fail to realize their full potential, we are all diminished. My fervent wish for anyone who explores this book: May you have a *Best Self Circle*—a circle of support for your personal growth—for the rest of your life.

UBUNTU 2

Part One

Chapter 1
Meditation

Stillness is the language that God speaks. Everything else is a poor translation.

— Rumi

This is a photo of gymnast Simone Biles meditating just before one of her competitions at the 2024 Olympic Games.

You'll remember that Simone backed out of the final round of the gymnastics competition in the 2020 Olympics because she experienced what gymnasts call the "Twisties." That's when a gymnast becomes disoriented in midair during their routines.

Through meditation, she was able to reduce the "negative talk" in her mind and focus on what she had practiced through years of training.

In the same way, meditation helps to reduce the thinking activity in the mind and, by doing so, gives you a choice of how to respond to situations rather than react out of fear, old habits, or past conditioning.

Here's Buddhist monk Thich Nhat Hanh explaining the science of meditation.

Thich Nath Hanh on the Science of meditation 3

This book begins by focusing on the cultivation of stillness through meditation, an indispensable tool for crafting a truly wonderful life. For me, meditation has been central to developing a healthy and strong relationship with every dimension of my life. In this book, meditation will be the crucible in which great wisdom and insights are forged. That's because meditation opens a portal into the realm of Universal or Natural Intelligence.

At the beginning of every meditation training, I ask participants to close their eyes and hold their breath for 90 seconds. Most people can't do it. They begin to feel pressure in the back of their throat, the lungs, the stomach, and the chest. Some people even feel as though they're suffocating or drowning. But no matter how clever their strategy or how resolute their will, the impulse to breathe always wins out.

The exercise is intended to physically demonstrate that there is a force or intelligence greater than our individual intelligence and will that is ultimately controlling our lives. It's commonly called Universal or Natural Intelligence. Universal because everything in existence is controlled by this force, and Natural because it is not conceived, activated, or controlled by the human mind. In fact, this greater intelligence actually created the human mind. By connecting more fully with this supreme force or intelligence, we connect to an expanded dimension of reality.

Scientists from Einstein (**Unified Field Theory 4**) to David Bohm (**Implicate & Explicate Order 5**) have come to appreciate the power and presence of this Universal Intelligence. It was Einstein who said: "I want to know the mind of God. Everything else is a detail." The "mind of God" speaks to this greater intelligence which is timeless, ever-present, and ever-conscious. This is what meditation connects us to.

Most humans access only a fraction of their intellectual capacity. Meditation expands and strengthens the ability to access the full range of our intelligence, including Universal Intelligence. This matters because all of the qualities that make life worth living, such as creativity, insight, curiosity, love, joy, and meaning, all emanate from Universal Intelligence.

Here's the tricky part: You can't fully access Universal Intelligence only by thinking about or studying it because pure Consciousness is beyond thought. The 17th-century French philosopher René Descartes' fundamental proof of existence was ***"I think therefore I am," 6...*** establishing thought as the highest determinant of human existence. For hundreds of years since, this pronouncement has been the foundational reasoning for Western intellectual, technological, scientific, and psychological principles—even to this day.

But then the 20th-century French philosopher Jean-Paul Sartre came along to posit: ***"I am aware of my thoughts, therefore I am"7.*** This insight represents a radical paradigm shift in recognizing that thought is not the ultimate arbiter of reality—awareness or pure Consciousness is. Mind-blowing, isn't it?

That means, when air is flowing into and out of our body, it's not our thinking mind making it happen but rather Universal Intelligence that permeates and animates not just our body but also the entire cosmos. Again, meditation connects us to this limitless realm.

Ironically, the hardest aspect of meditation for us humans is trusting that it is very much a natural process. Two long-standing meditation aphorisms are, "Whatever happens in meditation is your meditation" and "Meditation teaches meditation." They mean that the biggest obstacle to meditation is our own judgment about what we think should happen rather than simply accepting our actual meditation experience as meditation itself, no matter the form it takes. We start "shoulding" all over ourselves. And yet, the more we meditate with no expectation of outcomes, the more it guides and firmly connects us to our own limitless potential.

By repeatedly tapping into pure awareness through meditation, we reboot our perception and experience of who we really are. We discover that "We are not human beings having a spiritual experience, but rather spiritual beings having a human experience" (Pierre Teilhard de Chardin). Our perceptions shift into a new and expanded awareness of ourselves.

Tat Tvam Asi 8 is the Sanskrit pronouncement of "You Are That." It means that everything in the universe is created, permeated, and animated by this one Universal Intelligence, including us humans. Meditation is the first step toward separating thought (Descartes) from awareness (Sartre). Through meditation, each time we become aware of our thoughts, we are, in fact, connecting to this limitless potential.

What are the inherent qualities or characteristics of Universal Intelligence? They are:

AWARENESS: Contained in everything in the cosmos and beyond, from rocks to fish, to humans, to planets and stars, there is a dimension of ceaseless pure knowing. It's what enables a rock to maintain its "rockness" and a tree to maintain its "treeness." It is the human quality that enables you to experience "you as you" despite every cell in your body changing every seven days, or what makes you feel you are the same person at seven, seventeen, and seventy years of age.

ONENESS: Since Universal Intelligence is the force that creates, permeates, and animates everything in the universe and beyond, it can never experience separateness. Therefore, it can never act against itself because there is nothing but itself.

LOVE: The essence of love is becoming conscious/aware of this oneness as we relate to other people, places, things, ideas, etc. We often describe this phenomenon as feeling a connection to another person or thing. People often experience this connection with another person, while being in Nature, or being so absorbed in an activity that time and personal identity completely dissolve. Love is also unconditional in its giving and receiving, just as in Nature. Think air, water, sunlight.

JOY/BLISS: The natural state of Universal Intelligence is joy/bliss. Because it is complete unto itself, Consciousness cannot experience fear, anger, greed, loss, prestige, or any other emotions tied to the human experience. Universal Intelligence, in its purest form, can only experience a sense of complete contentment or peace... out of which flows joy/bliss.

TIMELESSNESS: For Universal Intelligence, there is no "clock time," only the present moment. This is why we humans always feel the same internally, even though our bodies show signs of aging... as does everything else in the temporal world. This is why reflecting on the past or anticipating the future can only happen in the present moment.

Yogis, mystics, philosophers, and poets have known about this timeless universal dimension for thousands of years. They use many names for this Intelligence such as: Mother Nature, Gaia, Tao, Brahman, God, and Buddha Nature, just to name a few. And if you're a Star Wars fan, you might even call it the Force.

Science is just catching up to these insights. In his book *Stillness Speaks*, Eckhart Tolle sums up the nature of this Universal Intelligence and its impact on human interactions:

"What Buddhists have always known, physicists now confirm: there are no isolated things or events. Underneath the surface appearance, all things are interconnected, are part of the totality of the cosmos that has brought about the form that this moment takes. When you say 'yes' to what is, you become aligned with the power and intelligence of Life itself. Only then can you become an agent for positive change in the world."

In a way, what we're attempting in this book is the science of spirituality—practices that, when done in a certain way and with a certain frequency, will yield a range of predictable outcomes. So, rather than unquestioned belief, you're invited to engage your curiosity in a disciplined investigation. It's as though we are conducting a series of subtle experiments where our body, mind, and spirit are the laboratory. At times, there will be various passages quoted in this book from wisdom literature to underscore the timeless and profound effects of these practices, which have been known for thousands of years.

In classic meditation, there are four primary areas of focus: **Body, Breath, Mind, and Mantra.**

BODY:

The body is the primary instrument used for meditation. Through the body, we experience physical sensations as well as the mental and emotional activity that can either facilitate or hinder our meditation process. For that reason, it's important that the body is made as comfortable as possible so it doesn't become a distraction.

First is the sitting posture. For those who practice Hatha Yoga, a common position is to sit on the floor in a half-lotus or full-lotus posture, often with a cushion under the sitting bones of the buttocks. The spine is straight but not rigid, with your hands resting on your knees or thighs, palms either up or down. Some yogis like to keep their hands in **chin mudra 9**, with the thumb and index finger touching on each hand. The jaw is relaxed by creating a slight space between the upper and lower teeth, allowing just the tiniest tip of the tongue into the space. The tongue then rests on the floor of the mouth. Eyes are closed and yet still looking straight ahead as though peering into a dark cave. The chin is slightly elevated, which will help prevent falling asleep during meditation.

In a chair, again the back is straight. Sometimes, a cushion supporting the back against the chair can be helpful. Another option is to place small cushions under each thigh, which presses the spine comfortably against the back of the chair. Feet are flat on the floor with knees about shoulder-width apart. Again, the hands are placed comfortably on the thighs or knees, palms either up or down. The jaw is relaxed, the tongue on the floor of the mouth, chin slightly elevated, eyes closed and looking straight ahead.

It is possible to meditate lying down, but it requires a few extra steps. First, in a lying posture, place a rolled-up towel under the curve or nape of the neck. Adjust the thickness of the towel to ensure there is no strain on the neck. A helpful indicator is that the back of the head is touching the floor, bed, or sofa. Next, place a cushion under each knee to ensure there is no excess strain either on the knees or the lower back while keeping the spine straight. And again, the jaw is relaxed, the chin will automatically lift because of the rolled-up towel, and eyes are closed and looking straight ahead. Hands are at your sides with palms facing either up or down.

The one big precaution for lying meditation is that you must make sure you are fully rested before attempting this posture. Since lying down is the normal sleeping posture, the body can easily slip into sleep mode during meditation if you are the slightest bit tired, which defeats the goal of staying fully conscious.

BREATH:

Your breath is the vehicle that carries you to the full realization of your Best Self—the doorway to Universal Consciousness. It is the instrument you will use to distinguish between thought and awareness, which most people mistakenly think are one and the same. That's because the breath is one of the most tangible manifestations of the pure consciousness animating every aspect of human existence (remember the 90-second breath exercise mentioned earlier). In classic meditation practice, it's the breath that deserves our full attention.

MIND:

The human mind is arguably the most complex and powerful instrument in the phenomenal world. From the mind has come all of the human advances in existence. One estimate is that the mind captures and processes approximately 11 million bits of sensory impressions every second.

And yet, the wise ones—and now scientists—posit that there is another dimension of intelligence beyond the human mind: pure consciousness. It is that consciousness or awareness that we are striving to experience through meditation.

And yet, knowing the power of the mind, it's extremely important not to fight the mind nor to be drawn in by thoughts during meditation. Instead, we simply keep redirecting our attention to something other than the thoughts produced by the mind... and that's where the mantra comes in.

MANTRA:

A mantra can be a word or phrase we repeat to focus our attention on something other than our thoughts during meditation.

It can also be the key that opens the door to a totally new reality. In many spiritual traditions, the mantra serves as a constant reminder of the goal of meditation: a complete connection with Universal Intelligence.

Some spiritual teachers suggest reading certain scriptures, poems, or quotations as a mantra, by repeating them daily in a slow and highly focused way for 10, 15, or 20 minutes each day. Popular examples are *The Serenity Prayer*, *Prayer of Saint Francis*, chapters of the *Bhagavad Gita*, and many more.

Many mantras are commonly used for meditation in various traditional spiritual practices, such as: *Om Mani Padme Hum* (Buddhist), *Om Namah Shivaya* (Hindu), *Wei Wu Wei* (Taoist), and *The Lord's Prayer* (Christian).

Another common mantra device is to become absorbed in the sounds of natural instruments such as singing bowls, hand cymbals, wind chimes, and the bamboo flute. I often teach this form of meditation by comparing listening to these instruments to *sound surfing*. Just as surfers ride waves into the shore, meditators are invited to mentally ride the sound of these instruments until it dissolves into silence; repeating this technique each time the singing bowl and chimes are struck or the flute is played.

And yet, the most consistent, powerful, and pervasive mantra is the breath itself. Focusing on the inhalation and exhalation of the breath, and the slight gap of silence in between the breaths, has been an indispensable and reliable mantra for millennia.

I personally enjoy focusing on the gap, especially between the exhalation and the inhalation. In that gap, there is no thought, so that all we experience is pure awareness. The gap is very short, so I confess to sometimes slightly pausing my breath there just to prolong the sweet experience of the "no thought" moment.

The Mind as a Psychic Instrument

To understand what's happening in meditation, we first have to understand more deeply how the mind operates. For that, I'm going to try and divide the most complex instrument on the planet into three distinct parts: The Thinking Mind, Awareness, and Will.

The **Thinking Mind** produces thoughts. It captures and categorizes information and sensations from the phenomenal world, stores memories and emotions, and retrieves this data when needed. It also has the ability to anticipate future events and remember past events. The thinking mind is by far the most dominant and recognizable aspect of the mind.

Next is **Awareness**, which makes us conscious of what's going on around us. This aspect of the mind is significant because it is the means by which we ultimately recognize and experience Universal Intelligence—because it *is* Universal Intelligence. It's the one aspect of the mind that has the capacity to shift between the sensory world and formless consciousness.

Then there is the **Will**, which determines where to focus or direct our attention and awareness. Because awareness and attention are constantly fluctuating among thoughts, emotions, and sensations, it is often very difficult for the Will to stay focused on pure consciousness for any significant amount of time. How often have you heard people say their mind is running all over the place?

So, the basic practice of meditation is a slow and deliberate effort to strengthen our Will so that it can remain aware of Universal Intelligence for longer and longer periods of time. It's like deciding where to point a flashlight in a dark room. While a gross oversimplification, hopefully, this model explains how the mind functions during meditation.

The Meditation Process:

The next step is to coordinate the flow of these processes to achieve a meditation experience. First, if possible, find a room or a space that is dedicated exclusively to your meditation practice. If that's not possible, then try to use the same space every day. In this way, the body and mind become accustomed to the space and glide more easily into meditation. The room should be clean, uncluttered, and well-ventilated, with some type of window treatment to block harsh light. The temperature in the room should be more on the cool side, even if it means using a shawl or light blanket for meditation. Some people place incense or a pleasant fragrance in the room, which can make the meditation experience more inviting.

Then assume your preferred posture and repeat your preferred mantra—whether it's the sound of singing bowls, a quotation, a traditional mantra, or simply the breath. Inhale and exhale normally through the nose. If possible, breathe from the abdomen, which allows for a fuller breath. As meditation unfolds, thoughts will invariably come up. Again, rather than resisting the thinking mind or being absorbed in a barrage of thoughts, simply redirect (Will) your attention back to your chosen mantra. And that's the work: continually redirecting your attention away from your thoughts and back to your chosen mantra.

For beginning meditators, I recommend starting with a 10-minute meditation at the same time and place every day. As the practice gets more comfortable, gradually increase the time to 30 minutes of meditation a day, which is an excellent place to stabilize an ongoing practice.

While meditation may be simple, it's not always pleasant. In this relaxed state, certain feelings and experiences that we have suppressed for years will begin to surface. Carl Jung calls these suppressed impressions **The Shadow**, and Eckhart Tolle calls it **The Pain Body**. The hard work is allowing these thoughts and feelings to come up without offering any resistance. By allowing them to arise while continuing with your meditation process, we begin to realize they are simply old thoughts and fears that no longer need to control us unless we give them the emotional power to do so. Over time, fear, sadness, regret, trauma, and emotional pain begin to subside, which is one of the tremendous gifts of meditation. There is a Yoga Sutra that says, *True courage is facing your fears and watching them back away.*

One of the great gifts of meditation for me has been the ability to dredge up these unconscious or suppressed fears, anger, and self-esteem issues that haunted me for much of my life. Though not pleasant, I've managed to allow them to surface in meditation and then to dissolve. I don't fully understand the alchemy of how it happened; only that it has. I do know that by making these unconscious impressions conscious, these emotional agonies no longer have control over me.

The best example for me is when I was in the third grade. My teacher and parents considered me to be functionally illiterate and unteachable. They didn't think I deserved any meaningful investment in academic development. I went on to graduate second in my high school class and was offered dozens of college scholarships, including several from Ivy League universities. And yet, many years later, somewhere deep in my subconscious and despite plenty of evidence to the contrary, I still wondered if that third-grade judgment might be true. As a result, I often reflexively acted out of that insecurity. Through meditation and the constant discipline of self-love and care, that judgment no longer holds any power over me. However, I did find the early years of my meditation daunting for this very reason. But it was worth the effort. Courage, perseverance, patience, and compassion for myself and others, I find, are essential tools for becoming free from the emotional baggage of the past through meditation.

My Approach to Meditation

My meditation practice starts normally between 5:00 and 5:30 each morning. I sit in a chair and go through the four stages of my practice.

Stage 1: I listen to or read some inspirational writings that remind me of aspects of life that are extremely meaningful to me. Examples of my preferred texts are Eckhart Tolle's **Stillness Speaks 10,** Eknath Easwaran's commentary on the **Bhagavad Gita 11** and Pema Chödrön's **How We Live is How We Die 12.** They are constant reminders for me that Universal Intelligence and I are one and the same. Though profoundly rich and insightful, I consciously make no effort to analyze, reflect on, or think about these texts during my meditation. I trust my Natural Intelligence to process the information in a way that is most useful to me. Sometimes, it can be weeks, months, or even years before I gain what I consider to be profound insights into a particular section of a text. And that's okay. Patience and perseverance are key.

Stage 2: I sit in silence for about one hour, watching the inhalation and exhalation of my breath combined with the sound of the mantra **HamSa 13** with each breath. *HamSa* is called an *ajapa japa* mantra, which means that rather than consciously repeating it, this mantra repeats itself through the sound of the breath. Therefore, I'm listening to the sound of *HamSa* with each breath rather than intentionally repeating it. *Ham* on the inhalation. *Sa* on the exhalation. A slight pause in the gap between the breaths, then repeat. *HamSa* means "I Am That" Universal Intelligence.

Stage 3: I listen to a recording of Tibetan Singing Bowls for about 15 minutes, which helps me to comfortably transition out of deep meditation and back into my normal thinking activity. For this, I use headphones or earbuds to listen. I also turn down the volume as low as possible while still being able to hear the sound of the singing bowls. This technique helps me to focus more deeply on the sound of the singing bowl.

The two recordings I use most often are:

Chakra Tune-up With Himalayan Bowls 14

Redwood Tingsha Meditation 15

Both can be found on YouTube and are produced by Temple Sounds.

Stage 4: I journal after meditation to capture any insights or feelings that may have come up during meditation or activities from the previous day. It's purely a stream-of-consciousness process. I often end my journaling by listing three things I'm grateful for, which can run the gamut from the peacefulness of my meditation to an exceptional cup of chai to the fun I had playing with our dog Lola.

I can't stress enough how valuable journaling has been for me. In fact, most of this book has come from my years of journaling. For me, it refines my perceptions—not just in meditation but in every aspect of my life. In Part II of this book, we will explore the journaling process more fully.

My Meditation Experience

For me, meditation is an indispensable tool that guides me from ignorance to knowledge to wisdom of the Self or Universal Intelligence. The great 19th-century Indian mystic Ramakrishna explained the distinctions this way: *"Those who hear of fire are ignorant. Those who see fire are knowledgeable. Those who make fire and cook with it are wise."*

By this definition, to merely study Universal Intelligence, no matter how nuanced our understanding, is still ignorance. But one who has had a direct experience of the Supreme Reality is knowledgeable, and the one who can summon the experience of oneness at will is truly wise.

In more than 40 years of meditation practice, I've been fortunate enough to get glimpses of the more subtle levels of pure consciousness, and those glimpses have been enough to spur me on.

During my meditation, I pretty consistently feel a deep sense of contentment during what is normally about an hour-long meditation. For me, contentment means a feeling of complete satisfaction. I neither want nor need anything. No fears of future events. No regrets of past events. No judgments of myself or others. For me, another term for this kind of deep contentment is peace.

When I close my eyes in meditation, my inner vision is often filled with colored lights. I consider these lights to be reflections of the energy centers in the subtle body called chakras. There is an extensive body of research on **chakras 16** and the subtle body that is well worth studying. These lights can be dull or brilliant. They can be completely still like a fog, like slow-moving clouds, or like blobs in a '70s lava lamp. The colors can change from white to red, to indigo, to yellow, to blue-green like the Aurora Borealis.

I breathe normally from the abdomen using the mantra *HamSa*, which serves as a steady reminder of my true nature: *I Am That*. As thoughts come, I redirect my attention back to the lights or to the breath, which seems to absorb or dissolve the thoughts. Some minutes in, I experience a level of deep contentment that usually lasts throughout the meditation.

Often, I find that peace/contentment is only the beginning of my meditation experience. Depending on the day, it can also take me into deeper and deeper dimensions of the Self.

- Beyond contentment, there's physical pleasure.
- Beyond pleasure, there's joy.
- Beyond joy, there's insight/inspiration (*satori*).
- Beyond insight/inspiration, there's expansive love.
- Beyond love, there is no Lester; only pure awareness.

Here's a short meditation exercise by Eckhart Tolle using the breath.

Eckhart Tolle Meditation Practice 17

Chapter 2
Intention

In order to start, we must make a decision. This decision is a commitment to daily self-cultivation. We must make a strong connection to our inner selves. Outside matters are superfluous. Alone and naked, we negotiate all of life's travails. Therefore, we alone must make something of ourselves, transforming ourselves into the instruments for experiencing the deepest spiritual essence of life.

— *365 Tao Daily Meditations* by Deng Ming Dao

Nowhere can we exercise greater control than over our own lives. Unfortunately, most of us rely primarily on cues from our family and friends, our environment, and past experiences to decide how to live. Consequently, we live reflexively, relying on past conditioning to guide us in the present moment. However, to live a great life, we must first choose to live a more purposeful and conscious life by forming personal intentions. A personal intention is not about what we want to do but rather the kind of person we want to be throughout our life.

Personal intentions, particularly regarding love, fear, purpose, and death, are not about achieving distant goals but rather about living a chosen set of values and principles right now, in every moment. They are an inspirational call to action. One of the most famous intentions in history is attributed to Mahatma Gandhi, who said: "Be the change you want to see in the world." Ironically, it's by living our intentions in the present moment that we shape our destiny and change the world.

No Values... No Intention

Values are the very foundation of any intention. Our values chart the path we follow, either consciously or unconsciously. For any value to be truly viable, it's extremely important that we can clearly explain what effect it has on us and on those around us.

This image of an aquarium illustrates that point. It serves as a metaphor for any group—whether the family, the workplace, the community, the country, or even the world. It represents ecosystems where all of its inhabitants either thrive or suffer together. In an aquarium, the quality of life depends on clean air and water, an ample supply of food, as well as the absence or presence of predators and diseases. If the water in one part of the aquarium gets polluted, the entire aquarium gets polluted. Just think of the COVID pandemic as an example.

The same is true about the social and emotional aspects of ecosystems, too.

There are qualities that either enliven and enrich an environment... or attitudes and behaviors that degrade it. It all starts with consciously knowing and living our core values in every moment of every day.

Here's a link to a video by psychotherapist Larisa Halilović on the importance of identifying our core values:

Larisa Halilović on Finding your Values 18

You'll notice Dr. Halilović stressed how our core values highly influence the relationships around us. Again, that's why the aquarium metaphor is so critically important when considering our core values. If we only cultivate values that benefit us individually, then we aren't contributing to the health of our relationships or our community. If the larger society doesn't thrive, ultimately we all fail to fully thrive. Every ecosystem, every community, every culture in the entire world is an interdependent system. The world thrives or fails by what we contribute to and take from it.

I'm asking you to answer three essential questions as you formulate your top three core values:

1. **Define your value.** Make sure the definition is meaningful to you.

2. **Explain how this value serves you.** How does it move you to become the person you want to be?

3. **Explain how your value serves others.** How does it contribute to the larger community or culture?

One of my three personal values is *unconditional love.* Here's how I would answer these three questions regarding unconditional love.

DEFINE A CORE VALUE:

UNCONDITIONAL LOVE

For me, unconditional love has three essential elements:

1. *Wanting the best for someone and for myself.*
2. *A willingness to make sacrifices so that the "best" can be achieved.*
3. *Asking nothing in return for the sacrifices made.*

HOW DOES THIS VALUE SERVE YOU?

UNCONDITIONAL LOVE

My relationships are no longer transactional, and I can act purely from what I understand to be what's best for the situation. I now have a way to be supportive of everyone, even people with whom I strongly disagree or even dislike.

HOW DOES THIS VALUE SERVE OTHERS?

UNCONDITIONAL LOVE

Others will come to experience that I'm completely transparent with my words and actions and have no intention to manipulate them for some hidden agenda. In this way, people can trust what I say and do and know that I have their best interest embedded in every decision and action.

Values Exercise

That's one of mine. The question now is, what are your three most important values?

Here's the exercise:

1. Identify the three most meaningful values for yourself.
2. Answer the three essential questions for each value.

I suggest you identify your three values first before you start answering any of the three questions.

Here is a link to a list of values you can review. It's not an exhaustive list, but hopefully, it will stimulate your thinking:

Personal Values List - Break the Twitch 19

And here's a link to an online journal to begin capturing your work.

Sample online journal 20

FORMING YOUR INTENTION

Now that your core values are in place, you can begin to build your intention. This is where your values take the shape of a narrative that is uniquely meaningful and inspiring to you. Your intentions will determine how your values express themselves through the dimensions of love, fear, purpose, and death in your life.

As with your core values, when we form an intention, it must have three distinct aspects. First, it must be a clear articulation of your intention. This time, the definition will take the form of an active declarative statement. Second, you must be able to explain how and why this intention serves you. It should not be exclusively tied to acquiring personal power, prestige, or possessions. Those are goals rather than desired qualities of personal growth. Third, it should explain how and why it serves humanity and the planet. Without these three components, the intention is not fully life-affirming. A perfect intention is: "Thou shalt love thy neighbor as thyself." (*Matthew 22:34-40*)

Here are intention templates to use in forming all four of the intentions in this book:

INTENTION TEMPLATE FOR LOVE, FEAR, PURPOSE, AND DEATH

MY INTENTION IS:

(Write full intention)

____

____

THIS INTENTION SERVES ME BY:

(Explain)

____

____

THIS INTENTION SERVES HUMANITY AND/OR THE PLANET BY:

(Explain)

____

____

In the Appendix A of this book are intentions from well-known authors on love, fear, purpose, and death. You're invited to review them as a way to draw insights and inspiration for your intentions. Then take away whatever element really resonates for you—whether a word, phrase, or the entire quote—to form your intention. Most importantly, form an intention that inspires you to be your Best Self. Only you can know what that is.

Your intentions will be firmly grounded in you by slowly and deliberately reading all three aspects of one intention each day, continuously rotating through all four. Once a year, it's helpful to reexamine your intentions and their rationales to make sure they are still relevant and resonate with you. If they are not, then change them. In this way, your intentions mature as you do.

Chapter 3
Love

Your task is not to seek love,

But merely to seek and find all

The barriers within yourself that

You have built against it.

— Rumi

This is a male Emperor Penguin in Antarctica taking care of a penguin egg while the mother is off to the ocean feeding so that she can nourish her chick when it hatches. He must hold the egg on his feet for up to four months. The image illustrates the universal impulse to nurture, support, and protect in the animal world. That same impulse exists in every human being as well—it's called Love.

The one connecting thread through all the episodes of my life has been love, either its absence or its presence. My evolving understanding of love has certainly colored every relationship

I've ever had—from parents and wives to colleagues and teachers, to children and friends, and even adversaries. It has been the primary gauge for my sense of belonging or not belonging among people and circumstances. Since the word "love" was never even spoken in my childhood home, let alone discussed or physically expressed, I started my personal search for love with significant deficits.

As a teenager, I remember being captivated by the idea of love after listening to the lyrics of the Burt Bacharach/Hal David song, *Alfie*, sung by Dionne Warwick. The lyrics that grabbed me were:

> "As sure as I believe there's a heaven above, Alfie
> I know there's something much more
> Something even non-believers can believe in.
> I believe in love, Alfie
> Without true love we just exist, Alfie
> Until you find the love you've missed
> You're nothing, Alfie
> When you walk let your heart lead the way
> And you'll find love any day, Alfie."

The line that still grabs me to this day is: "Something even non-believers can believe in." To me, this version of love sounded both mysterious and unattainable, yet I was intrigued. So, my search began.

I immediately fell into the romantic trap of looking for my "soulmate" who would totally care for and completely accept me just as I am—complete me. My obligation in the relationship was to totally care for all of her needs and to make her happy. What I've since come to understand is that this kind of arrangement is not true love but rather a romantic version of *quid pro quo*, a transaction where each person expects to get what they want out of the relationship. Of course, when one person fails to live up to their part of the unspoken agreement, hurt, anger, and mistrust show up, putting a serious damper on the sweet feelings we mistakenly thought were the totality of love. With this brand of love, when the feeling is lost, often the relationship is lost. Cue the Righteous Brothers.

So, why does true love seem to constantly elude us?

Perhaps it's because we're looking for love in all the wrong places. Sometimes, we want to *be* loved more than we want to learn *how* to love. Maybe we think we should naturally *fall* in love with a person with whom we have the right chemistry. Maybe love *hurts* so much that we don't want to become too vulnerable. Maybe we think love is *finite* or limited, and since there's not enough to go around to everyone, it's better to save it just for our family and close friends. Maybe we think someone has to *earn* our love before we give it. All of these scenarios are actually barriers to ever experiencing true love.

Leo Tolstoy studied 100 religions and philosophies of the world and found the one common element to all of them was love, which led him to conclude: "Love is life. All, everything I understand, I understand only because I love. Everything is, everything exists, only because I love. Everything is united by it alone. Love is God, and to die means I, a particle of love, shall return to the general and eternal source." Based on my own experience, I've found that true love is both a noun and a verb: two complementary dimensions of the complete experience of love.

Love as a Noun

Take a moment to focus on someone you deeply cherish. Often, feelings of closeness, trust, passion, vulnerability, acceptance, and many more tender qualities arise. We often feel a deep sense of devotion and protection for that person, which could also be true for devotion to a cause or an organization.

This simple exercise reveals two important facts. First, love is a naturally occurring quality common to every human being. Second, we can tap into this state with no external stimulus. No one needs to be physically present, expressing their love to us, for us to fully experience strong feelings of love. Certainly, the memory of a loved one can trigger profound feelings of connection. However, the simple truth is that if we didn't inherently possess the capacity to love, those feelings could never arise in the first place.

Why is this true?

Only from the view of Universal Intelligence can we begin to get a clearer picture of love as an inherently human quality. From the perspective of pure Consciousness, there is nothing but itself; therefore, it can never act against itself. For example, we would never consider cutting off our legs or hands because we know they are a part of us. In the same way, Universal Consciousness supports all aspects of existence—from the grossest to the subtlest—even what we subjectively consider good and evil. The sun never makes a judgment of who does or doesn't deserve to receive its rays. It is unconditionally available to everything and everyone. This is how natural love operates.

For that reason, just as heat is the primary quality of the sun, love is the primary quality of Universal Consciousness—the experience of complete oneness and benevolence for all things. We experience loving qualities simply because it is our nature to feel them. The important understanding about love is that it naturally exists in every human being, and to seek it outside of ourselves is an exercise in futility. The great challenge and the hard work lie in removing the barriers in us and around us (Rumi) that inhibit our ability to fully experience the complete ecstasy of love. The hard work is learning how to be loving even when we're not feeling love and are actually feeling fear, anger, hate, and mistrust.

Love as a Verb

This brings us to love as a verb—an action; to *be* loving. It means that love is also a decision about how we choose to engage with others. Because it's a learnable skill, loving gets better with practice. According to a Yoga Sutra, any act of unconditional love aligns with three core principles:

Love is:

- Wanting the best for others and yourself.
- Demonstrating a willingness to make sacrifices so that the best can be achieved.
- Asking for nothing in return for the sacrifices made.

For me, the implications for this type of love are huge. It means there are no conditions or expectations attached to a genuine act of love. What matters most is that a desire for the well-being of someone else and yourself is enough. It means the feeling of love doesn't need to be present for us to be loving. In fact, we can proactively love people we don't even like (*love your enemies*). It means there's no need for reciprocal expressions of love or gratitude. It's no longer about someone deserving our love before we give it. And because we can show love to anyone, our capacity for loving is limitless. It means no matter how small or large, any gesture can be an expression of love: from running into a burning building to save a life to smiling at someone in the grocery store to picking up a piece of trash from the street. Another ancient Yoga Sutra says: "We don't love others for their sake alone. We love others for our sake."

Conversely, we can cause great emotional suffering for ourselves and others by withholding our love and compassion. When we limit our expressions of love out of fear, judgments, and expectations, we limit our ability to fully experience love, and inevitably, suffering follows. Mother Teresa expressed it very well and succinctly when she said: "Love until it hurts. When the hurt is gone, all that's left is love."

Here's the big payoff: The more we perform acts of love (*verb*), the more we actually experience the state of love (*noun*). Each feeds the other until all that's left is the experience of love. I think this is Mother Teresa's point.

Self-Love is Essential

While it's implied in this section, let me be very explicit. Self-love is a critical aspect of a complete love experience. We tend to seek love and affection outside ourselves because we don't know how to access it within ourselves. We don't understand that our very nature is love. Seeking love from others, at some point, is bound to cause only hurt and disappointment. I find unconditionally giving and receiving love and affection to myself first is a much healthier and more satisfying approach. The more I love and nurture myself, the more I'm capable of offering that same loving care to others.

Here's an extended excerpt from Anita Moorjani's book, , **Dying to be Me,** which I think powerfully illustrates this point:

"I now live my life from joy instead of fear. This is the one simple difference between who I was before my NDE (Near Death Experience) and who I am today.

Before, without even realizing it, everything I did was to avoid pain or to please other people. I was caught up in doing, pursuing, searching, and achieving; and I was the last person I ever took into consideration. My life was driven by fear—of displeasing others, of failing, of being selfish, and not being good enough. In my own head, I always fell short.

Since my NDE, I don't feel that I came back to accomplish anything. I only came back to be. Because of this, everything I do comes from love. I don't worry anymore about trying to get things right or comply with rules or doctrines. I just follow my heart and know that I can't go wrong when I do so. Ironically, I end up pleasing more people than my old self ever did, just because I'm so much happier and more liberated.

By letting go of any self-judgment, we allow our world to transform; and as it does so, we'll be able to feel greater and greater trust. The more we're able to trust, the more we're able to let go of trying to control the outcome. When we try to move with this flow rather than adhere dogmatically to the doctrine of others or the beliefs we once had that no longer serve us, we more accurately reflect who and what we truly are."

To conceptually understand and value these aspects of love is one thing; but to live the principles is quite another. This is where we must commit to becoming our own human laboratory—exercising acts of love in every moment. No small thing. To do that, I've created a template (page 53) for you to write your own love intention that will guide your interactions with every person and in every encounter. Remember, intentions are not about how you want to change the world. Rather, intentions are about how you choose to be in the world, consistent with your values.

As an example, here's my personal LOVE Intention inspired by the Prayer of Saint Francis:

My Love Intention is:
Let me be an instrument of peace.
May I not so much seek to be consoled but to console,
Not seek to be understood but to understand,
Not seek to be loved but to love.
For it is in giving that I receive,

It is in forgiving that I am forgiven.

This is how my presence lives on long after this body is gone.

My Love Intention Serves me by:

Reminding me that any act of love and compassion must begin with me and my motivation for action. It cultivates peace, joy, and courage in me because I know that I am offering my Best Self to others at every moment.

My Love Intention serves Humanity and the planet by:

Reinforcing with every person I encounter that they are worthy of love, not because of their actions, conditions, or status but simply because they are part of the ONE universal Intelligence that permeates and animates everything and everyone in existence. I extend my acts of love and compassion to the planet as well.

REMINDER: In the Appendix A of this book is a list of quotes from a variety of well-known texts and individuals to get you started on creating a Love intention for yourself. They are only intended to be thought starters, so feel free to take from them a word, a sentence, or even an attitude that really inspires you.

LOVE INTENTION TEMPLATE

MY LOVE INTENTION IS:

(Write full intention)

____

____

THIS LOVE INTENTION SERVES ME BY:

(Explain)

____

____

THIS LOVE INTENTION SERVES HUMANITY AND/OR THE PLANET BY:

(Explain)

____

____

Chapter 4
Fear

If you can face your fear, you will go beyond it. Then you will become completely fearless. If you hold yourself back because of fear, you will lose everything...

— Yoga Sutra

I n Indian folklore, there is an ancient parable called the "snake in a rope," which offers instruction on fear caused by misidentification. In dim light, it's easy to mistake a twisted rope for a coiled snake. If you imagine it to be a poisonous snake, your "fight, flight, or freeze" impulse kicks in. Heart rate becomes more rapid, corticosteroid levels elevate, perspiration increases, and blood flow to the legs intensifies—all in preparation to confront the impending threat of a poisonous snake. But as you get closer and the light grows brighter, you realize it's only a twisted rope that poses no threat to you at all.

Many wisdom texts suggest that this misidentification (*Maya 21*) is the source of so much unnecessary fear and suffering among humans. We often perceive a threat where there is none. So, the constant challenge for us is how to distinguish between real and imagined threats.

Let's begin with real threats. To be clear, fear is a very healthy response in certain situations, especially when bodily harm may be imminent and precautions should be taken. Going into a bomb shelter during a missile attack, running away from the sound of gunfire, or finding shelter during a hurricane are all situations when natural survival instincts appropriately kick in. Wild animals also experience these same natural responses to a threat. But unlike wild animals, which revert to a state of biochemical homeostasis or equilibrium after a threat has passed, humans tend to hold on to and even relive serious threats, sometimes for the rest of their lives, causing heightened levels of emotional and biochemical stress—even though the threat is gone. Hence, Post-Traumatic Stress Disorder (PTSD).

There are a multitude of ways to deal with these lingering traumas, such as positive psychology, traditional psychotherapy, and trauma-informed yoga practice, just to name a few. In dealing with personal traumas, I have found meditation to be highly effective.

Then there are imagined threats that trigger an unwarranted fear response. Once again, the anxiety is caused by misidentification or ego attachment to something or someone. Franciscan priest Richard Rohr reduces this misidentification to three specific areas: Power, Prestige, and Possessions. In all three areas, anxiety happens when we experience these aspects of our life as extensions of who we are and they appear under threat. In other words, any threat to our power, prestige, or possessions is tantamount to being physically and personally attacked.

Power speaks to having control over outcomes regarding personal circumstances, the behavior of other people, and the environment; extending or withholding approval; our opinions being highly valued, etc. This dynamic also speaks to a misidentification with a perceived lack of power, resulting in a feeling of victimhood.

Prestige speaks to giving priority to the opinions of others: how we are personally regarded in society by virtue of job or career status, accomplishments, family, race, sexual preference, perceived beauty, education, etc. At the heart of prestige is an attachment to the opinions of others, either positive or negative. Social media influencers are the latest iteration of our fanatical attachment to the opinions of others.

Possessions speak to one's level of attachment to physical items such as homes, cars, bodies, clothes, jewelry, etc.—or the lack thereof. It also speaks to the degree to which possessions either add to or diminish one's sense of power and prestige. Driving a late model Lexus projects one type of power and prestige. Driving a Ford Fusion projects a very different one.

These three distinctly human impulses also have a symbiotic relationship with one another, exponentially reinforcing misidentification. For example, the president of the United States lives in the White House, is accorded the finest amenities in the world, and routinely makes life-and-death decisions. Hence, the president exerts the ultimate in power, prestige, and possessions. Whereas a homeless person lives in a tent under a bridge, digs for food out of garbage cans, and is often ignored on the street. And yet, each person has a heart that beats and lungs that breathe by virtue of Universal Intelligence. Each one will die, and then their power, prestige, and possessions will mean nothing to them.

In either situation, the degree of ego attachment to these external conditions and circumstances ultimately determines the level of fear and suffering a person experiences.

When dealing with fear, there are at least three antidotes: Detachment, Awareness, and Intention.

Detachment: Cultivate the understanding that there is a greater you beyond your power, prestige, and possessions—even beyond your thoughts. Understand that all you have will someday be taken away, either by circumstance or by death, and yet all of these things combined can never measure up to your true greatness. Every person has multiple identities, which will ultimately dissolve. Reflecting on this truth helps to let go of power, prestige, and possessions and points to who you are beyond these ego identities.

In terms of detachment from the opinions of others, writer and lecturer Brené Brown offers this wise advice:

> "The opposite of belonging is fitting in. Because 'fitting in' is assessing a group of people and thinking, *Who do I need to be? What do I need to say? What do I need to wear? How do I need to act?*—and then changing who you are. True belonging never asks us to change who we are. It demands that we be who we are. Because if we 'fit in' because of how we've changed ourselves, that's not belonging. Because you've betrayed yourself for other people. And that's not sustainable because you start to lose yourself. And the minute I become who you want me to be in order to fit in and make sure people like me is the moment I no longer belong anywhere."

Awareness: Being fully attentive in the present moment is an excellent tool to train the mind to slow down and see what's happening before responding. It provides that split second to not react but rather to choose how to respond to a situation (*Intention*). Ask yourself: *"Is the challenge in this moment a threat to me physically or merely a threat to some aspect of my perceived power, prestige, or possessions, all of which will ultimately dissolve anyway?"* When fear comes up, through awareness, we can breathe slowly to give ourselves emotional space. Then ask ourselves, *"What's the most useful and loving response I can offer to this situation?"*

One practice I've found enormously helpful is applying **The Four Gateways of Speech.** They are:

- Is what I'm about to say **true** or only my opinion?
- Is what I'm about to say **kind** and respectful?
- Is what I'm about to say **timely** so that others can fully digest what I'm saying?
- Is what I'm about to say **beneficial** to the question or situation at hand?

Walking through these four questions with awareness makes our comments impeccable. Integrity is when our thoughts, words, and actions are in complete alignment.

Intention: Consciously choosing how to respond to a given situation rather than reacting to it out of habit and unconscious conditioning is intention. It offers both choice and agency. Intention acknowledges and accepts circumstances as they are, yet it offers us the freedom to respond out of our closely held values rather than anxiety or irritation. That's why it's critical that we form intentions that point to our greatness beyond our power, prestige, and possessions.

Here's the example of my Fear Intention:

My Fear Intention is:

Love dissolves fear. May I have the courage to choose the most loving response in every situation, no matter how afraid I might be.

My Fear Intention serves me by:

Reminding me that at the heart of my spiritual practice is constantly making choices between love and fear. I consciously choose love over fear because love is stronger and more life-affirming than fear.

My Fear Intention serves Humanity and the Planet by:

Acting in harmony with the highest principles of Universal Intelligence, my every action is in harmony with Natural Intelligence, positively affirming people and the planet.

Again, a reminder that there are many examples of Fear Intentions in the appendix to browse and draw inspiration.

FEAR INTENTION TEMPLATE

MY FEAR INTENTION IS:

(Write full Intention)

____

____

THIS FEAR INTENTION SERVES ME BY:

(Explain)

____

____

THIS FEAR INTENTION SERVES HUMANITY AND/OR THE PLANET BY:

(Explain)

____

____

Chapter 5
Purpose

Work is love made visible. And when you work with love, you bind yourself to yourself and to one another and to God.

— *Kahlil Gibran*

This tree growing out of a rock physically illustrates the twin goals of purpose. First and foremost, the tree strives to become what it is intended to be—a fully developed tree despite the harsh conditions that make such growth seemingly impossible. And second, the tree then offers its gifts back to the surrounding environment: branches for birds to nest, leaves for animals and insects to eat, clean air to breathe.

In the same way, there are two levels of purpose for every human being: Universal and Individual. Unless these two levels of purpose are cultivated and aligned, we can never achieve the full potential of our humanity. At the universal level, every human being's highest purpose is to know their Self and then serve humanity and the planet. This principle is very evident in Nature, like our tree, where all things strive to fully become themselves and then offer back to the larger ecosystem in their own unique way—whether plankton feeding whales or bees pollinating plants. No living thing can exist in total isolation. Only by giving to and receiving from the larger ecosystem can all of Nature survive and thrive.

You'll notice in the preceding paragraph that the "S" is capitalized. That's because this Self is not about the sensory-driven identity such as male or female, American or European or Latin, tall or short, learned or unlearned, etc. This Self speaks to having a connection to Universal Intelligence. It means constantly cultivating that connection through prayer, meditation, selfless service, being in Nature, or countless other ways. It can be any practice that stills the activity of the mind so a person can experience pure consciousness, which permeates and activates everything.

Ram Dass, the Harvard professor turned spiritual teacher, tells the story of a woman who attended one of his lectures. He described her as a very modestly dressed woman wearing a simple hat, guessing that she was perhaps a homemaker.

In the lecture, as he began to describe the more and more subtle realms of his experiences of pure consciousness, he noticed that the woman would nod knowingly, suggesting that she had similar experiences. Her knowing nods continued throughout the lecture.

Finally, at the end of his talk, Ram Dass approached the woman to ask how she seemed to understand these esoteric states that had taken him years of practice with psychedelics, scriptural study, meditation, selfless service, and yoga to achieve. She simply replied, "Oh, I crochet."

Whatever stills the mind and gives you a glimpse of your limitless potential is a sacred practice.

There's also a famous Buddhist Koan that says:

- *Before enlightenment, I chopped wood and carried water.*
- *After enlightenment, I chopped wood and carried water.*

The only thing that has changed between the two actions, before and after enlightenment, is the understanding of "I." Before enlightenment, "I" is the physical person egocentrically performing all of the actions. After enlightenment, "I" is both the understanding and the experience that all actions spring from the one source, Universal Intelligence or pure consciousness.

It means living from a firm conviction that you are so much more than your acquired power, prestige, and possessions. You need not look to these acquisitions or achievements to define your worth. Rather, it's out of the fullness of who you truly are that you serve humanity and the planet.

The Second Aspect of Universal Purpose

Whatever service is rendered, it needs to emanate from a place of love in action as much as possible. Remember the three criteria for any true act of love:

- Wanting the best for someone and yourself.
- A willingness to make sacrifices in order that the best outcome is achieved.
- Asking for nothing in return for the sacrifices made.

In Sanskrit, this type of service is called *seva* or selfless service. Any concern about praise or blame, advantage or disadvantage, only diminishes the power of the service rendered. However, the more we serve from a place of unconditional love, the greater the connection to a personal experience of the Higher Self. Pure acts of love are the highest expression of Universal Intelligence. *"God is Love"* (John 4:16).

Individual Purpose

Now, speaking to Individual Purpose, it becomes a matter of what drives and inspires you. It's essential that Individual Purpose aligns with our Universal Purpose to be most effective. That means it must be of service to people and the planet as well as to ourselves. Eckhart Tolle calls it *awakened doing*. He offers a unique framework within which we perform any action, whether large or small:

"The modalities (attitudes) of awakened doing are Acceptance, Enjoyment, and Enthusiasm. You need to be vigilant to make sure that one of them operates whenever you are engaged in doing anything at all—from the most simple task to the most complex. Modality means the underlying energy frequency that flows into what you do and connects your actions with the awakened consciousness that is emerging into this world."

— A New Earth, Eckhart Tolle

Acceptance: Through this attitude, we find the capacity to perform large and small tasks that we find either unpleasant or uninteresting. Think of changing a flat tire, cleaning the bathroom, or weeding the garden. While not our preferred activity, we understand that the effort is necessary to achieve a greater goal such as driving our car, using a sanitary bathroom, or allowing flowers and vegetables to grow weed-free. Tolle stresses that it's important we understand why we're performing any given task for it to be meaningful. If we can't perform the work with at least acceptance, he suggests we shouldn't do it at all, because otherwise, we are not taking responsibility for our life. We are allowing ourselves to remain unconscious of the consequences of our actions.

Enjoyment: Through this attitude, we engage with activities that bring us joy and pleasure, no matter how simple or grand they may be. The activity itself is its own reward. "Clock time disappears, and you are fully present in the activity. The common misperception of enjoyment is that it springs from what we do when it actually connects us to our innate joy. Activities that we like merely trigger our internal joy, much like priming a pump. It removes the barriers that keep us from fully experiencing our own joy. Acts of enjoyment are done for their own sake, not for any future outcome or gain.

Enthusiasm: This is performing acts of enjoyment with a particular goal in mind. For example, an artist may open an art studio to share their love of art. Another example is NBA phenom Steph Curry, who shares his love of basketball by offering personal and financial support to women's basketball programs at both the amateur and professional levels. The trick with enthusiastic action is to not be attached to the outcome of a goal. Yes, set goals, but also be surrendered to a different outcome. Being attached to the outcome of a goal diminishes the joy of the effort and only increases the stress and anxiety for the giver.

The Purpose of Purpose

Coming from a limited sense of self, purpose is often used to provide meaning and identity for a person. It gives them the chance to demonstrate how they are productive and contributing members of society, which helps them to gauge their value in that society. However, that identification rises and falls based on the opinions of others. This approach to purpose certainly has value because it serves as both an emotional growth opportunity for the giver and provides some tangible benefit to society. However, this is not the highest realization of purpose.

Coming from a fullness of Self, the highest realization of purpose is the opportunity for an individual to selflessly give from their gifts acquired in life, both physical and experiential, which are life-affirming for humanity and the planet. This type of enthusiastic, purposeful giving or selfless service reinforces the sheer joy of conscious giving as well as reaffirms one's innate value, which requires no external validation.

My Purpose Intention is:

"Don't ask what the world needs. Ask what makes you come alive and go do it. Because what the world needs is people who have come alive."

— Howard Thurman

My Purpose Intention serves me by:

Challenging me to find and connect with those facets of my life that bring me the greatest joy and meaning. Then actively cultivating those aspects of my life to ultimately offer those talents and skills to humanity and the planet.

My Purpose Intention serves humanity and the planet by:

Urging me to give that which I find most precious within myself to humanity and the planet.

Once again, a reminder that a list of quotes on *Purpose* can be found in the appendix.

PURPOSE INTENTION TEMPLATE

MY PURPOSE INTENTION IS:

(Write full Intention)

____

____

THIS PURPOSE INTENTION SERVES ME BY:

(Explain)

____

____

THIS PURPOSE INTENTION SERVES HUMANITY AND/OR THE PLANET BY:

(Explain)

____

____

Chapter 6
Death

"People who run from death and those who run to death suffer from the same problem. They don't know how to live."

— James Finley

This is a photo I took of a florist shop window in Venice, Italy. Flowers are often used as a metaphor for the transience of life. We can witness their life cycle from growing to blossoming and to withering within a few days or weeks. It shows us the natural and inevitable life cycle for every human being. Denial is delusional. In the Buddhist tradition, flowers represent the impermanence of all living things and all actions.

There's a great final scene in the movie **Scent of a Woman 22** starring Al Pacino, who plays a grandfather on his deathbed surrounded by his wife and children. Suddenly, his young grandson rushes in and asks, "What's wrong with Grandpa?" The grandmother calmly replies, "Nothing, dear. He's just dying."

The scene runs so counter to how most of us in the West talk about and think about death. For most of us, death is a problem to be fought until the bitter end.

There is a Buddhist principle: *"When we resist what is, we suffer."*

What does it take to overcome our fear of death and to die in peace? One answer can be found by addressing the three perennial questions people ask when they think about death and dying:

1. How do I deal with the process of dying?
2. What happens to me at the moment of death?
3. What will happen to me after I die?

I went to Ram Dass's book, **Still Here** for some answers. In fact, many of my comments on death are inspired by his book because I think Ram Dass has both eloquently and practically captured the dynamics of death as a result of supporting hundreds of people through their dying process.

1. How do I deal with the process of dying?

The great challenge in dying is letting go of everything we're attached to on this side of the phenomenal curtain: our bodies, our minds, our family, friends, possessions, joys, regrets, resentments... The list is endless. That's because none of these things—physical, mental, or emotional—can go with us.

There's a great story of a Mongol warlord in the time of Genghis Khan who was famous for the treasure he had amassed from pillaging cities and towns across Asia and Eastern Europe. But on the day of his funeral, he ordered that his hands be exposed outside his coffin, facing upward, as his body was paraded through the streets on the way to his burial site. His intention was to show the world that for all the wealth he had amassed, he could take nothing with him into the afterlife.

One answer to the first question is to *die before you die*, or as Plato put it, *practice dying*. One reliable way is through meditation: constantly letting go of thoughts and emotions while returning our attention again and again to the breath or the mantra. When you let go of your attachment to your power, prestige, and possessions—as well as the anxieties that may come up in meditation—you are directly preparing to "drop the body," as the expression goes in India. You stand in the place of an observer, allowing these sensations to arise and dissolve with no attachment or aversion to them.

This experience reminds me of a quote from the Dalai Lama, who often says, *"Today is a good day to die."* I take that to mean he has released all things that bind him to this material world, and he is peacefully prepared to move into the next realm.

2. What happens to me at the moment of death?

This is the point at which the physiological changes in the body accelerate. First, the senses begin to close down: loss of taste, blurred vision, muffled hearing, etc. According to the ***Tibetan Book of the Dead 23,*** the elements of Earth, Air, Fire, and Water begin to recede from the body.

For this reason, I am eternally grateful for the HamSa mantra. It's called a *chaitanya* mantra, which means it is pure consciousness in the form of the mantra. *HamSa* means "I am That." It vibrates at the frequency of Universal Intelligence, so the more we use the mantra, the more closely we resonate with pure consciousness. One of the great gifts of this mantra is that, in the moments just before death, it serves as a vehicle transporting the user toward death, easing the process of letting go of all things temporal while moving forward peacefully. But again, the point is to use the mantra *now* so that, in the final moments of dying, the mantra will arise effortlessly and transport you. As mentioned earlier, mantras can take many forms. It's about choosing the one that works best for you.

Great mystics like Gandhi and Neem Karoli Baba famously used their mantras throughout their lives and in the final moments of their death.

Not surprisingly, Ram Dass's answer to this question is the same: be prepared by getting our house in order now so that we can meet the moment of death with greater equanimity. Meditation and Intention. Meditation and Intention. Meditation and Intention. These are two highly recommended tools used by saints, mystics, and regular practitioners in preparation for death.

3. What happens to me after I die?

As Ram Dass explains, it depends on our level of spiritual evolution. If you're asking whether Lester Strong, the distinct personality, will continue to exist, the answer seems to be clearly no. And there's the anguishing rub for many people who are attached to their body, mind, and unique personality.

But if we have come to recognize that we are the same as Universal Intelligence—or the Soul or God—and if we understand that this Universal Force existed long before time and will continue forever, then we can feel reasonably assured that life continues in some form. Whether it's reincarnation in the Hindu and Buddhist traditions or Heaven and Hell for the Christians or the Mansions in the Kabala, virtually every religion has some explanation for the afterlife.

But perhaps the most important aspect of a peaceful death is living a full life *now*. It only stands to reason that the more we live by the principles contained within our intentions, the more aligned we will be with those principles even in death. I had a chance to interview B.F. Skinner, the great behavioral scientist and Harvard professor, just before he died. I asked him that, while he was an atheist, he seemed to be accepting his death with such calm and equanimity. He said it was true because he had lived his life fully and made contributions to the world to the best of his ability. So like the Dalai Lama, whenever death came, it was a good day to die for him.

Here is my *Death* Intention which is inspired by the story of the Mongol warlord.

My Death Intention is:

To all the people whom I have loved and who have loved me,

With gratitude, I now release them.

To all the people who have hurt me and whom I have hurt,

With gratitude, I now release them.

To this body, all its senses, emotions, and thoughts that have served me,

With gratitude, I now release them.

To all the prestige, power, and possessions which have served me,

With gratitude, I now release them.

I now embrace all aspects of my transition and move to the next stage of my journey in peace.

May it be so.

My Death Intention serves me by:

Reducing any anxiety over the inevitability of death and my attachment to things which I must release. I am then free to be fully present with my lived experiences here and now.

My Death Intention serves humanity and the planet by:

Serving as a model of calm acceptance of death and how death invariably unfolds in all of nature.

Once again, as you write, a reminder that a list of quotes on death can be found in the appendix.

DEATH INTENTION TEMPLATE

MY DEATH INTENTION IS:

(Write full intention)

____

____

THIS DEATH INTENTION SERVES ME BY:

(Explain)

____

____

THIS DEATH INTENTION SERVES HUMANITY AND/OR THE PLANET BY:

(Explain)

____

____

Part Two

CASE STUDIES FOR REFLECTION AND JOURNALING

Remember, some of the most profound words coming from this book are the ones that you write. They reveal your state of awareness at a given time and, on reflection, reveal your spiritual growth over time. The topic questions are only there to stimulate your thinking. What's most important is that you journal what is resonating and most relevant for you at the moment... always looking through the lens of your four intentions.

YOUR DAILY JOURNAL
Sample online journal

Chapter 7
An Antidote For Blaming And Shaming

Overview

The first question is: Why do people blame and shame others in the first place?

There are at least two common answers. The first is that people don't want to be personally blamed or shamed. So, they try to avoid being a target of ridicule by targeting someone else or something else.

The second reason is because people believe someone or something has threatened their view of how the world should operate... like those damn politicians in Washington.

The underlying emotion of both approaches is fear. Fear that the criticisms about us might actually be true and we actually deserve the scorn. Or fear that our world will become more uncertain, unrecognizable, and hostile to us.

As with most aspects of human development, we first have to heal ourselves before we can help to heal others.

Both Don Miguel Ruiz and Deepak Chopra offer remedies that have proven to be effective for millennia.

In his book, ***The Four Agreements 24***, Ruiz admonishes us to not take what people say or do to us personally. He asserts that no matter how hostile someone is towards us—even threatening to kill us—their actions have little to nothing to do with us.

They are simply acting out of their own perception of the world and the conditioning in their lives. Every person is the director of their own drama, and the rest of us are simply playing bit parts.

In his book, ***The Seven Spiritual Laws of Success 25***, Deepak Chopra says there are three essential attitudes we must assume in order to not be held hostage to the opinions of others and to difficult circumstances. He says:

1. "I will practice Acceptance. Today I will accept people, situations, circumstances, and events as they occur. I will know that this moment is as it should be, because the whole universe is as it should be. I will not struggle against the whole universe by struggling against this moment. My acceptance is total and complete. I accept things as they are at this moment, not as I wish they were." (My personal caveat on this: Acceptance does not mean resignation. It simply means having a crystal-clear and dispassionate view of the circumstances in front of you.)

2. "Having accepted things as they are, I will take
   Responsibility for my situation and for all those
   events I see as problems. I know that taking
   responsibility means not blaming anyone or anything
   for my situation (and this includes myself). I also
   know that every problem is an opportunity in
   disguise, and this alertness to opportunities allows me
   to take this moment and transform it into a greater
   benefit."

3. "Today my awareness will remain established in
   Defenselessness. I will relinquish the need to defend
   my point of view. I will feel no need to convince or
   persuade others to accept my point of view. I will
   remain open to all points of view and not be rigidly
   attached to any one of them."

Let me stress that these intentions are certainly not easy... and you may not even agree with them. Here's where you can be a spiritual scientist by testing these principles in your own life and seeing what results.

So, now that we have proposed ways to inoculate ourselves against shame and blame, how do we keep from blaming and shaming others?

For Miguel Ruiz, he recommends that you be impeccable with your words. He says that our words have enormous—even divine—power, which can either heal or destroy another person. He strongly believes we infect others with emotional poison through our negative words.

For that reason, he says it's vital that we choose our words very carefully.

A mindful practice that comes from a number of different traditions is called: **The Four Gateways of Speech.** There are four questions we're encouraged to ask ourselves before we speak, especially in difficult situations.

The Four Question Gateways Are:

Is what I'm about to say True?

Meaning, is it factually verifiable, or is it simply an opinion? Informed opinions can be valuable, but it's important to claim them as just that... opinions, and not assert them as fact.

Is what I'm about to say Kind?

Meaning, what is the most compassionate and respectful way for me to convey these facts? How do we focus on the situation at hand without shaming or blaming any person?

Is this the right Time and Place for me to raise this issue?

Meaning, can the other person or persons properly hear and digest what I'm about to say? Am I the right person to convey this message at this moment?

Is what I'm about to say Beneficial?

Meaning, how will my comments make a situation or a person's circumstances better? If it's just about personal venting with no real benefit to anyone else, then it's probably best to remain silent.

JOURNAL QUESTIONS

First, think about which of these comments you agree or disagree with and why.

Second, think of someone that you recently blamed for something (large or small), whether out loud or silently, and try to determine what troubled you about the situation.

Third, how would you convey your concern to that person using the Four Gateways of Speech?

Chapter 8
In Defense Of Optimism

Overview

Some of the most recent opinion polls found that more than 70% of Americans feel our country (USA) is headed in the wrong direction and that democracy is under threat.

Faith in our institutions like Congress, the Supreme Court, public schools, and the media is at unprecedented and historic lows.

Scientists predict that our climate will reach irreversibly catastrophic levels by the end of this century unless dramatic interventions are implemented now.

The wars in Ukraine and Gaza could spill over into World War III with the slightest miscalculation.

Against these dystopian scenarios, how can we possibly feel optimistic?

Well, it all depends on the lens we choose to look through.

If we choose to look only through the lens of world events, there is plenty to make us feel fearful, angry, and helpless.

That's because we're measuring our sense of well-being by things over which we have little or no control.

Catastrophic events have plagued humanity since the beginning of human existence.

The scholar and mystic J. Krishnamurti put it this way:

"In the search for power (or control), we are (trying to escape) a deep sense of frustration and fear – fear of life, fear of being uncertain, fear of death, fear of non-existence, and the fear which has been instilled in us through the organized religions of belief. They have always created a sense of apprehension, a sense that you have to be saved by an external power, symbolized in a human being or in certain ideas. This has created in man – who is after all the result of centuries of development from the animal, and is still the animal – a sense of fear, which has been inculcated and sustained."

In the realm of **Positive Psychology 26**, expecting the worst outcome and looking for and hoping for relief outside of ourselves is called catastrophizing. Two positive psychologists from UCLA and the University of Virginia challenged this notion by using a Robert F. Kennedy quote which reads:

> The gross national product does not allow for the health of our children, the quality of their education, or the joy of their play. It does not include the beauty of our poetry or the strength of our marriages; it measures neither our wit nor our courage; neither our wisdom nor our learning; neither our compassion nor our devo-

tion to our country; it measures everything, in short, except that which makes life worthwhile.

— (Kennedy, 1968)

Bottom line, general psychology since WWII has focused on our mental illnesses and trauma but has failed to capture the qualities that are inherent in every human being and from which we derive pleasure, healthy human engagement, and meaning. Positive psychology does.

Martin Seligman, one of the founders of positive psychology, offers these suggestions for cultivating each of these three life dimensions.

- **On Pleasure**, he suggests finding ways to do the things that we find pleasurable but cautions against the "ice cream" effect—meaning the more we indulge in pleasurable things, the less pleasurable they become. One ice cream cone tastes great; ten in a row don't.
- **On Engagement**, he talks a lot about what he calls the *Flow* state that's common among athletes, artists, and writers, which is when we become so immersed in a person or activity that we lose a sense of time and space. This can happen in relationships (especially loving relationships), work, or play. One way to achieve this state is to identify our greatest talents and skills and then reshape our relationships, work, and play to incorporate our greatest strengths.
- **On Meaning**, he emphasizes using our greatest talents and skills in service to others. He cites acts of

kindness and offering gratitude to others. On a scale of
most to least effective, Seligman says acts of meaning
are the most powerful prescription for happiness,
followed by engagement. He says pleasure has the
least lasting and beneficial quality.

JOURNAL QUESTIONS

Where do you need to put your attention to derive more joy in
your life?
Pleasure, Engagement, or Meaning

What are two of your greatest talents and skills, and how can
you use them to serve others?

How can you incorporate your greatest strengths into
Relationships, Work, and Play?

Chapter 9
Doing vs Being

Overview

The great Buddhist koan says:

"Before enlightenment, I chopped wood and carried water. After enlightenment, I chopped wood and carried water."

The only thing that changes within the action is the "I."

Before conscious awakening, "I" speaks to the ego-centered, sensory-driven "I," which is dominated by fear and desire: *What am I going to get or what am I going to lose by taking this action or making this decision?*

After conscious awakening, "I" speaks to the Universal "I," which is integrated into and animates everything in the universe and beyond. The Universal "I" (Buddha Nature) has neither fear nor desire. It can only BE itself because THERE IS

NOTHING BUT ITSELF. The Universal "I" is the source of insight-intelligence, creativity, love, peace, joy, and so much more.

So, rather than the question of DOING vs. BEING, I suggest the best approach is **DOING WHILE BEING.** The more we can expand and strengthen the connection between our ego-self and our Universal Self, the greater our actions and decisions will be influenced by our deepest wisdom and compassion.

The seemingly insurmountable challenge, however, is that most of us aren't enlightened. As a result, we constantly default to old habits, behaviors, and ways of thinking. This is where the values within our Intention can serve us so powerfully. If done correctly, these values are life-affirming—that is to say, they seek to enhance the quality of life for us, humanity, and the planet. And since every universal principle expresses or manifests the same Intention, we become more and more aligned with our Universal Self through every action and decision we make.

My core values are **Unconditional Love, Presence, and Defenselessness.** I also find that meditation both strengthens and enhances my Intention and my connection to the Universal "I." And of course, the "Carnegie Hall" mantra is the cardinal rule here:

Practice, Practice, Practice.

JOURNAL QUESTIONS

Do you agree or disagree with this approach of "Doing and Being?" Please explain.

What values currently guide your actions and decisions?

How can you ensure you will act from your values, especially in high-stress situations?

Chapter 10
Living Without Regrets

Overview

In looking back on the regrets in my life, the common thread through all of them was fear. Fear of being rejected, fear of appearing inadequate, fear of embarrassing myself— and on and on. As a result, out of a state of fear, I would choose the safer option rather than the option my heart and intuition said was the best for me. That's when regret comes in for me, because I knew better.

This is where a bit of self-compassion is necessary. Otherwise, the regret would haunt me for the rest of my life. Eckhart Tolle's perspective is helpful in this regard. He makes the point that, given our maturity, understanding, and life conditions at that time, there was literally no other decision we could have made. So it's important to forgive ourselves.

How do we not make the same mistake going forward? For me,

it's about making decisions from a place of love rather than fear. It's remembering my fear intention, which is:

Love dissolves fear. May I have the courage to choose the most loving response in every situation no matter how afraid I might be.

As a result, the more I act from a place of love, the more I experience the state of love, which is presence, tenderness, trust, and connection with other people and with my higher Self. Mother Teresa said it well:

"Love until it hurts. And when the hurt is gone, all that's left is love."

JOURNAL QUESTIONS

What is your current relationship to regrets?

How can you make peace with your past regrets?

Is there someone you know who is a role model for self-forgiveness?

Chapter 11
Transitions

"DON'T CRY BECAUSE IT'S OVER. SMILE BECAUSE IT HAPPENED."

— DR. SEUSS

Overview

Basically, every human being has to find ways to navigate changes in their lives, large and small, good and bad. Otherwise, we mindlessly move from one circumstance to another, trapped on an emotional rollercoaster—hurdling constantly from celebration to depression, from stability to upheaval.

There are essentially three stages to every transition: **order**, **disorder**, and **reorder**. To effectively manage these stages, it's important to prepare ourselves to peacefully coexist in each of them.

First is Order: This is when there is a period of relative predictability in our situation, whether good or bad: marriage, child-rearing, current job, and so on. In these relatively stable moments, it's vital to understand that change is still coming—it's inevitable and unavoidable. Couples part, children leave home, and jobs change. Emotions will undoubtedly accompany those changes: happiness, sadness, fear.

These moments of stability are the best times to prepare for eventual and inevitable change. We can appreciate the experience for what it is—and learn from it, good or bad, so there are no regrets once it's over. Next, we accept the experience for what it is, only an experience, and not a definition of who we are. Nothing that is temporary can ever truly define us.

It's in this stage that our need and desire for stability and predictability can cause us to try to hold onto what has been, which can become a source of greater suffering as we try to resist change.

Second is Disorder: I think it was Michelle Obama who said, "Being president doesn't change who you are. It reveals who you are." In the same way, when we are confronted with upheaval and challenge, our core values will become even more evident, not less.

The opportunity is for us to become well-established in our most treasured values now, so that when inevitable changes come, we are prepared to meet them with our best selves.

In these moments of instability, well-developed and practiced values will serve and protect you.

Third is Reorder: Socrates said, "The secret of change is to focus all your energy not on fighting the old, but on building the new."

The key word here is adaptability—it's the Darwinian imperative: embracing what is versus what was. We can't drive forward very well by looking through the rearview mirror.

This also addresses the long-standing question of whether adaptability or acceptance of what is equates to resignation of the current condition. The answer, once again, is of course not. However, it does mean surviving, and hopefully—if we've done our work—thriving in the newly formed circumstance, whether pleasant or unpleasant.

It invites us to lean into how we may grow, deepen, and awaken to affect the quality of life we ultimately seek.

JOURNAL QUESTIONS

How did you cope with a major transition in your life?

What resources supported you, and what did you learn about yourself?

Would any of these recommended stages have supported that transition? How?

Which of the three stages do you find most challenging and why?

Chapter 12
Resolution And Reconciliation

Overview

Recently, I was asked to list words that captured my feelings moments after a presentation about the chaos in Gaza and Israel. I wrote **Resolution** and **Reconciliation**.

Resolution because I expect events in the Middle East to get worse before they get better, frankly, and that regardless of the intensity of the conflict, my commitment is to live from a place of love and compassion. I can appreciate how "Pollyanna" that may sound to some people, especially in the face of the unspeakable atrocities we've already seen and heard.

And yet, in my little corner of the world, I choose to put my trust and energy in love and compassion. **Resolution** because I know that my conviction is going to be tested over and over again as I watch the news and talk with family, friends, and neighbors.

Reconciliation because compassion requires me to meet people where they are—in their pain, their outrage, and their despair.

In a larger context, there have been countless atrocities comparable to these in the past, and sadly, there may be even more horrendous ones yet to come. I see my work as standing in that breach, in some small way, serving as what Buckminster Fuller called "the cosmic glue" that holds this fractured world together through love and compassion.

JOURNAL QUESTIONS

What's your approach for dealing with horrific incidents both at home and abroad?

How do you find peace in the midst of the chaos?

Chapter 13
When The Dancer Becomes The Dance

Overview

I recently watched the women's and men's NCAA Final Four college basketball tournaments and was totally blown away by the incredible grace and skill of those athletes. Having been a player myself, nowhere near this skill level, I marveled at how "thinking" was only a fraction of what was on display. It was more about instinct and muscle memory from years and years of intense practice that was really on display.

In an ashram where I lived for many years, there was a framed aphorism on the wall that read: "Only one who obeys can command," pointing us to understand and, perhaps more importantly, to experience what it means to be in alignment with the laws that govern the universe. Whether it's the Bible, the Koran, *A Course in Miracles*, or the *Tao Te Ching*, they're all urging us to come into alignment with the guiding principles of the universe. And by being so intimately connected to them, it's impossible to distinguish the dancer from the dance —Consciousness from the awakened person.

That is why Nature is such a wonderful teacher for us. Birds don't have to study aerodynamics to fly. They just instinctively fly. Flowers don't have to study botany to grow. They just grow. All of Nature is showing us in countless ways every day that this kind of alignment is possible. But we big-brained humans must consciously give ourselves to intense study and practice in order to recapture what is inherently our natural birthright. And when we enter that Zone or Flow, effort becomes superfluous. Awakening to our full human and divine potential is, to me, our greatest opportunity and our greatest challenge.

JOURNAL QUESTIONS

Have you ever had an experience that so completely allowed you to lose yourself in it, stay in that present moment, and experience joy?

Have you ever considered such a moment to be a spiritual experience?

What do you need to do to rekindle such experiences?

Chapter 14
The Gift Of Mistakes

By our stumblings, the world is perfected...

— Sri Aurobindo

Overview

I love this quote from Sri Aurobindo.

Mistakes and missteps are not only a fact of life; they are essential to our growth.

From babies walking, falling, and getting up, to Edison's 25,000 failures while inventing the light bulb, to the NASA tragedies with the space program—mistakes pave the way forward.

So, why are mistakes so hard to accept when they happen to us personally?

Often, it's because we see our mistakes as a criticism and indictment of who we are.

Rather than thinking "I made a mistake," too often we think, "I *am* a mistake" (Brené Brown).

We fail to understand that our actions are about what we do—not about who we are.

As a result, we often hear criticism from others as a personal attack on us. Only when we can move beyond self-criticism and the criticism of others can we truly experience the gifts our mistakes can give us.

For me, this is why one of my core values is **Defenselessness**.

It's a term coined by Deepak Chopra in his book, *The Seven Spiritual Laws of Success*.

It means: "*I will relinquish the need to defend my point of view. I will feel no need to convince or persuade others to accept my point of view. I will remain open to all points of view and not be rigidly attached to any of them.*"

Another critical factor for me in getting the most out of my mistakes is having a sense of the core values that guide my life.

They are my North Star.

I once heard the late Senator Ted Kennedy talk about his love of sailing and the incredible importance of tacking.

He said that while he always knew where he was going, the wind and waves would invariably knock him off course, so he was constantly turning the bow of his boat into the wind to change direction.

He loved it.

But it was only possible because he knew his ultimate destination.

Living in a way that enables me to be my best self is my lighthouse.

JOURNAL QUESTIONS

What is the hardest part of accepting your mistakes, and why?

What is your process for dealing with mistakes?

Chapter 15
The Tyranny Of Judgment

Overview

At their core, judgments are comparisons of what *is* to what we think *should be*. We all make countless judgments every day—it's part of the human condition. However, suffering sets in when we become so attached to our judgments of what *should be* that we cannot accept what *is*. As a result, we block our own joy or satisfaction. There are at least two fallacies to this line of thinking.

THE FIRST FALLACY is that somehow people or circumstances should adapt to the way you think, which, of course, is wholly delusional. And in that delusion, there is suffering for you, not for others.

THE SECOND FALLACY is that your joy and happiness are tied directly to external circumstances. But the truth is that your capacity for joy, peace, and love is inherent to you—not to the world.

The great teacher of these two points is nature, in the forms of sunlight and water.

Sunlight, because it makes no judgments about who will or won't receive its rays, shines equally on everyone and everything. Sunshine is always sunshine—radiating heat and light, its inherent qualities, regardless of what's occurring in the cosmos.

Water, like sunlight, always maintains its inherent integrity and has the additional quality of adaptability—taking the form of solid, liquid, or gas, plus the ability to take the shape of any container, from a drinking glass to an ocean to a glacier.

So how does all this translate to human judgments?

First, like sunlight, we are able to be with anyone in any circumstance and still maintain our inner qualities of love, joy, and peace.

And like water, we can adapt while holding to our integrity. The challenge and opportunity are to figure out what love, presence, and defenselessness (my three core values) look like in any situation.

Finally, it's recognizing that every person and situation is like the three states of water: solid, liquid, and gas. It is not my responsibility to change the state but rather to accept it with unconditional love, presence, and defenselessness. Every person has the capacity to change states—frozen in a hardened view of their life circumstances, liquid in their ability to adapt to circumstances, and gaseous, which is to transcend the vagaries of everyday life and tap into their inherent love, joy, and wisdom.

JOURNAL QUESTIONS

How often do your judgments of people and situations cause you frustration or anxiety?

What are you going to do about it?

Is there a particular area of judgment you would like to focus your attention on?

Chapter 16
Bending The Blue Line

Overview

I have a friend and neighbor who I consider to be a technological futurist and ethicist. For months now, he has been poring over the emergence of technologies as far back as the invention of the wheel to the present moment and analyzing how those technologies have impacted humanity, both helpfully and destructively.

He showed me the trend lines for the continued development of both technology and humanity—and it scares him. He observes that the accelerated development of technology over the next 20 years will be exponentially faster than human development. The inevitable outcome, as he fears, is humanity becoming subservient to technology.

He sent me one of those "New Yorker" style jokes where an AI system is talking to its programmer through a monitor.

The AI system says: "I'm only here to collaborate with you to get the best results."

Then the programmer says: "Great, what would you like for me to do?"

And the AI system says: "Well, you can clean the dust off my monitor and empty the wastebasket."

UGHH!

On his graph, a red line represents the rapid "hockey stick" growth of technology, while the meandering blue line represents human growth. The yawning gap between the two lines represents the level of dominance of technology over humanity.

We need look no further than biomedical technology (vaccines, cloning), military technology (attack drones, Patriot defense systems, hydrogen bombs), and social media technology (TikTok, YouTube, Facebook, Instagram) to see the trendline for how these technologies are influencing or even controlling the psyche of humanity.

His question for me—and now my question for you—is: how do we bend the blue line so that human development keeps pace with or even exceeds technological development?

I certainly don't have the answer, but I do think I may have some parts of an answer:

1. We human beings need to understand that we are so much more than an information processor. In fact, we are intimately connected to the Universal Intelligence that gave rise to all of these technologies and more.

Technology, in my view, is only a shadow of the pure
potentiality (Deepak Chopra) or the infinite creativity
of Universal Intelligence. Technology can only
capture, replicate, process, and extrapolate form—
considering thought to be form. But pure
consciousness, or Universal Intelligence, is formless. It
is what Einstein called: "The mind of God."

2. As a result, we human beings have the capacity to
imagine and conceive things that were seemingly
inconceivable—like these advanced technologies, for
example.

3. And finally, it is completely impossible for the creator
of a technology to become subservient to the creations
of technology. The problem is thinking that humans
are the creator rather than Universal Intelligence
itself... flowing through humans.

The great challenge for all of humanity is to connect with the
pure potentiality in us—that *is* us.

JOURNAL QUESTIONS

What are the ingredients of human potentiality (infinite
creativity) that are beyond the grasp of technology?

What does it look like for you?

Can you describe a personal experience of great insight or
creativity that had nothing to do with technology?

Chapter 17
The Dichotomy Of Relationships

"Engagement with humans can be Hell, or a great spiritual practice."

— Eckhart Tolle

Overview

Relationships, both personal and professional, can be demoralizing and fulfilling. They unquestionably shape our view of ourselves and the world. That is why we've labeled this topic *The Dichotomy of Relationships.*

Couples therapist Esther Perel, whose guidance we're following in this treatment, would say that it's through the challenges of relationships that we grow the most.

It is in those challenges that trust is either strengthened or lost.

Please watch this Perel video examining the fundamental dimensions of both personal and professional relationships:

Esther Perel Video 27

JOURNAL QUESTIONS

How well do you tolerate disconnections in relationships?

What process do you use to repair relationships?

What role do the factors of?
Complementarity,
Power dynamics,
Care & closeness (trust),
Respect & recognition

Play in navigating your relationships? Explain.

How do your values factor into your relationships?

Chapter 18
Leonard Cohen
In Search of the Sacred

Leonard Cohen singing Hallelujah 28

Overview

A 79-year-old singer/songwriter with a questionable voice, a self-described minor poet, an ardent student of the Torah, an insatiable lover, an alcoholic, a six-year resident of a Buddhist monastery, and the author of one of the most iconic songs in the world: *Hallelujah.*

This treatment is a look at Cohen and the song *Hallelujah* today because they strive for what every earnest spiritual seeker works so hard to do: to reconcile the sacred and the secular aspects of life.

In fact, some of Cohen's lyrics suggest that we find the sacred in the secular aspects of life.

The formal definition of *Hallelujah* is an expression of praise, joy, and thanks. So, what is Cohen saying to us when he sings about a "broken Hallelujah"?

Here's a bit more of Cohen walking the line between sacred and secular.

Leonard Cohen PBS Interview 29

Maybe his song Hallelujah is a celebration of imperfection. As a practicing Buddhist, perhaps Cohen embraced the Japanese Zen philosophy of **wabi sabi 30** which honors impermanence, imperfection, and simplicity, three qualities which characterized much of Cohen's life

JOURNAL QUESTIONS

What do you take from Cohen's *Hallelujah*?

How do you personally walk the line between the sacred and the secular aspects of your life... or are they the same to you? Please explain.

Chapter 19
Embracing Reality

Overview

We're exploring the work of Byron Katie Mitchell and her book *Loving What is 31*.

Her central point is that all human suffering comes from not accepting reality—seeing things not as they are but as we want them to be.

She's very emphatic about the point that acceptance is not resignation to a situation but rather honestly and dispassionately assessing a situation and then acting based on that clear assessment.

She says that when we stop opposing reality, our actions become simple, fluid, kind, and fearless.

She stresses that staying in your own business means gaining clarity on situations that we can affect and those we can't. The opening lines of the Serenity Prayer express this best:

*"God grant me the serenity to accept the things I cannot change,
The courage to change the things I can,
And the wisdom to know the difference."*

Her contention is that there are only three kinds of business in the universe: *My Business, Your Business,* and *God's Business.*

God's Business includes everything that is out of everyone's control, such as death, gravity, or planets and stars orbiting and colliding with one another.

Suffering happens, she says, when we mentally start living outside of our own personal business. We start "shoulding" all over everything.

When we think someone we know should be in a better relationship or a better job... or when we think there should not be wars, hunger, or impending annihilation through climate change, she contends that's when we're in somebody else's business.

Again, she stresses that we can always do what is within our control, such as voting for lawmakers who we think can best guide us away from war and famine, or recycling our metals and plastics and reducing our carbon footprint.

Katie Mitchell would say that if we are feeling stress, anger, or anxiety, we first need to ask ourselves, *"Whose business am I in?"*

Katie Mitchell says another ongoing struggle for people is understanding that we are not our thoughts, which are a product of past experiences and conditioning. The following excerpt explores meeting our thoughts with compassionate understanding:

> "A thought is harmless unless we believe it. It's not our thoughts, but the attachment to our thoughts, that causes suffering. Attaching to a thought means believing that it's true, without inquiring. A belief is a thought that we've been attaching to, often for years. Most people think that they are what their thoughts tell them they are. Thoughts just appear. They come out of nothing and go back to nothing, like clouds moving across the empty sky. They come to pass, not to stay. There is no harm in them until we attach to them as if they were true."

— Byron Katie Mitchell

JOURNAL QUESTIONS

Can you identify a time when you stressed about a situation over which you had no control?

How did you deal with it?

What is your relationship to your thoughts?

What is the greatest challenge posed by your thoughts?

Chapter 20
Is There A New Kind Of American Patriotism?

Overview

After watching the Democratic and Republican National Conventions, the recurring question of *"Who is a patriot?"* resurfaced for me. I confess my tortured history with the idea of my patriotism to America.

Given the legacy of slavery in America and my personal experience with racism in this country, it should be easy to understand why I and many other Black Americans do not hold this country close to our bosoms. For most of my life, the best attitude I could muster toward America has been transactional. I pay my taxes, give eight years of military service, and behave as a law-abiding citizen. In return, I get a great college education and exhilarating jobs that have allowed me to take care of my family. And yet, even though I was born and raised in this country, most often I feel like an outsider—institutionally tolerated but not always welcomed or embraced.

NBA coach Doc Rivers said it best after the George Floyd killing: *"We love America, but America didn't love us back."*

And yet, during the conventions, there they were—people of different colors, nationalities, genders, gender identities, and economic classes enthusiastically waving "Old Glory" and chanting *"USA, USA."* What was I missing?

The idea of *"Proud to be an American"* still doesn't sit well with me. It suggests too strongly that my dominant identity is wrapped up in my Americanness, which it is not. In the same way, my principal identity is not tied to my race, my gender, or my ancestry.

"Grateful to be an American" seems to fit a little better. Grateful for the extraordinary quality of life that my family and I have been blessed to experience. Having traveled to many countries around the world, I know how desperate circumstances can be for others. Think Gaza/Israel, Ukraine, Syria, and Sudan.

I'm grateful that I've been given the chance to use my talents and skills to make circumstances better for those around me. And finally, I am even grateful for the hard times I've endured in this country, which have given me the emotional strength to forge ahead despite setbacks.

I have the freedom to object when I consider something is going wrong. I have the right—and even the responsibility—to correct conditions I consider unsafe and unfair. I can even say that I love America because I do want what's best for her, and I'm willing to make sacrifices to help make the best happen. While I rarely feel warm and fuzzy feelings about institutional America, I do feel great love for many of her people—who, at the end of the day, are the real America.

Recently, Pat and I agreed to put an American flag on the front of our house as a reminder of the gratitude and love we feel for this very flawed but amazing country. For me, the flag is a celebration of both the promise and potential of America.

So, that's my process. What's yours? What kind of patriot are you—or do you consider yourself a patriot at all?

JOURNAL QUESTIONS

How would you describe your brand of patriotism? What does being an American mean to you personally?

What values and ideals define the promise of America for you?

How does being an American square with being a citizen of the world?

Chapter 21
The Stillness Imperative

Overview

From the earliest wisdom literature, stillness is held up as the principal portal through which we can fully experience pure consciousness, Universal Intelligence, or God.

"The goal of meditation is to still the activity of the mind."

— Patanjali's *Yoga Sutras*

"Be still and know that I am God."

— Psalms 46:10

"Stillness is the language that God speaks. Everything else is a poor translation."

— Rumi

Here is a more extensive quote that explains why stillness is so essential to experiencing the ultimate Reality:

"True stillness comes naturally from moments of solitude where we allow our minds to settle. Just as water seeks its own level, the mind will gravitate toward the holy. Muddy water will become clear if allowed to stand undisturbed, and so too will the mind if it is allowed to be still. Neither water nor the moon make any effort to achieve a reflection. In the same way, meditation will be natural and immediate."

— *365 Tao: Daily Meditations* by Deng Ming-Dao

I love talking about the movie *Salmon Fishing in the Yemen*, where a Yemeni Sultan decides to create a salmon-stocked stream in Yemen for sport. Though there are many problems with weather, soil, and geography, the REALLY BIG problem is with the salmon themselves. Since it was impossible to find enough wild salmon to stock the stream, they had to use farm-raised salmon. But farm-raised salmon have never swum upstream to spawn, creating the risk of the entire project becoming a massive failure. Desperate, they filled the stream with farm-raised salmon anyway—and lo and behold, the salmon intuitively started swimming upstream, and the entire project was a success.

I enjoy this story because, for me, it beautifully illustrates a powerful truth about us humans as well. Just like the salmon, if given the right conditions, our natural instincts kick in, enabling our True Nature to reveal itself. The right environment for us is a still mind, wherever we can find it: in nature, in meditation, or even in the shower. Silence is the environment most conducive to EXPERIENCING the state of Stillness. Stillness is essential to knowing our Universal Intelligence—that limitless force that creates, permeates, and animates everything in the cosmos and beyond, from the planets to a blade of grass.

To be clear, silence and stillness are not the same. Silence is the environment we create by removing as much internal and external noise as possible. Stillness, however, is a tranquil and thought-free state that is natural to every living thing. We become silent to experience the stillness that already exists within us.

JOURNAL QUESTIONS

In what ways do you struggle with being still?

Have you ever been able to connect with your inner stillness amid challenging circumstances?

What positive experiences have you had from being in Stillness?

Chapter 22
LOVE IS...

Overview

The inspirations for this title, *Loving is...*, comes from a quote by Leo Tolstoy. After studying approximately 100 religions and philosophies of the world, he writes:

"Love is life. All, everything that I understand, I understand only because I love. Everything is, everything exists, only because I love. Everything is united by it alone. Love is God, and to die means that I, a particle of love, shall return to the general and eternal source."

For me, it's only possible to grasp the magnitude of Tolstoy's view of love by both understanding and experiencing the infinite scope of pure Consciousness. That's because, from the view of pure Consciousness there is nothing but Itself. Therefore, pure Consciousness recognizes and experiences every aspect of the material world, from a blade of grass to the orbiting planets..., as itself. That's love.

It's also why the term "unconditional Love" is redundant. Love cannot be conditional because it is impossible to be transactional, *quid pro quo,* with itself. Kahlil Gibran said it beautifully in his poem *The Prophet.*

"Love takes not but from itself and gives not but to itself. For love is sufficient unto Love. And when you love, you should not say God is in my heart. Say rather that I am in the heart of God."

Therefore, lust, greed, anger, fear, judgment, hatred cannot exist in the space of pure love. That's why Tolstoy can confidently say *"Everything is, everything exists, only because I love."*

"only because I love." I think these four words are the most profound teaching in the entire quote. It says that Tolstoy didn't have this extraordinary experience of love by studying love.... but by acting and living from the space of love.

So, our questions center on what KEEPS US from fully experiencing love? We know every human being... in fact even wild animals have the capacity to love. Ironically, the primary person who suffers from our limited expressions of love is us. So, remember the three essential qualities of love:

• Wanting the best for someone and yourself.

• Demonstrating a willingness to make sacrifices to achieve the "best" outcome for everyone involved.

• Asking for nothing in return for the sacrifices made

JOURNAL QUESTIONS

Think of one person whom you strongly dislike and then ask yourself... "What behavior or attitude is keeping you from extending love to this person?

What needs to change for you to offer loving kindness to this person?

What's keeping you from doing it?

Appendix A - Quotes

LOVE INTENTIONS

"When making a decision, always choose the most loving option."

— Yoga Sutra

"Work (Service) is love made visible. And when you work with love, you bind yourself to yourself, and to one another, and to God."

— Kahlil Gibran

"Love God; then do what you will."

— St. Augustine

"With great respect and great love, I welcome you all with all my heart."

— Indian Sutra

"Love until it hurts. When the hurting stops, there is only love."

— Mother Teresa

Love gives naught but itself and takes naught but from itself. Love possesses not, nor would it be possessed; for love is sufficient unto love. When you love you should not say, "God is in my heart," but rather, "I am in the heart of God."

— The Prophet by Kahlil Gibran

"Your task is not to seek love, but merely to seek and find all the barriers within yourself that you have built against it."

— Rumi

God grant me the serenity to accept the things I cannot change,

The courage to change the things I can,

And the wisdom to know the difference.

Living one day at a time,

Enjoying one moment at a time,

Accepting hardship as the pathway to peace;

Taking, as Jesus did, this world as it is, not as I would have it;

Trusting that You will make all things right if I surrender to Your will;

So I may be reasonably happy in this life, and supremely happy with You in the next life. Amen.

— Reinhold Niebuhr

"Power without love is reckless and abusive, and love without power is sentimental and anemic. Power at its best is love implementing the demands of justice, and justice at its best is power correcting everything that stands against love."

— Martin Luther King, Jr.

"Life's most persistent and urgent question is, what are you doing for others?"

— Martin Luther King, Jr.

"My heart fills with loving-kindness. I love myself. May I be happy. May I be well. May I be peaceful. May I be free.

May all beings in my vicinity be happy. May they be well. May they be peaceful. May they be free.

May all beings in my city be happy. May they be well. May they be peaceful. May they be free.

May all beings in my state be happy. May they be well. May they be peaceful. May they be free.

May all beings in my country be happy. May they be well. May they be peaceful. May they be free.

May all beings on my continent be happy. May they be well. May they be peaceful. May they be free.

May all beings in my hemisphere be happy. May they be well. May they be peaceful. May they be free.

May all beings on planet Earth be happy. May they be well. May they be peaceful. May they be free.

May my parents be happy. May they be well. May they be peaceful. May they be free.

May all my friends be happy. May they be well. May they be peaceful. May they be free.

May all my enemies be happy. May they be well. May they be peaceful. May they be free.

May all beings in the Universe be happy. May they be well. May they be peaceful. May they be free.

If I have hurt anyone, knowingly or unknowingly, in thought, word, or deed, I ask for their forgiveness.

If anyone has hurt me, knowingly or unknowingly, in thought, word, or deed, I extend my forgiveness.

May all beings everywhere, whether near or far, whether known to me or unknown, be happy. May they be well. May they be peaceful. May they be free.

— Buddhist Prayer of Loving-Kindness

*"Lord, make me an instrument of your peace.

Where there is hatred, let me sow love;

Where there is injury, pardon;

Where there is doubt, faith;

Where there is despair, hope;

Where there is darkness, light;

Where there is sadness, joy.

O Divine Master, grant that I may not so much seek

To be consoled as to console,

To be understood as to understand,

To be loved as to love.

For it is in giving that we receive,

It is in pardoning that we are pardoned,

And it is in dying that we are born to eternal life. Amen."*

— Prayer of St. Francis

"To love is to recognize yourself in another."

— Eckhart Tolle

"Love is not selective, just as the light of the sun is not selective. It does not make one person special. It is not exclusive. Exclusivity is not the love of God but the 'love of

ego.' However, the intensity with which true love is felt can vary. There may be one person who reflects your love back to you more clearly and more intensely than others, and if that person feels the same toward you, it can be said that you are in a love relationship with him or her. The bond that connects you with that person is the same bond that connects you with the person sitting next to you on a bus, or with a bird, a tree, a flower. Only the degree of intensity with which it is felt differs."

— Eckhart Tolle

"Love is patient and kind; love does not envy or boast; it is not arrogant or rude. It does not insist on its own way; it is not irritable or resentful; it does not rejoice at wrong-doing but rejoices in the truth. Love bears all things, believes all things, hopes all things, endures all things. Love never ends."

— Matthew 1: 4-8

"To really serve, to really flourish, to have others flourish, you need to fall in love with something: with the seva (self-less service), the people you're working with, or the one for whom you work. There needs to be love. Without that chemical reaction, you become stale. So fall in love with your seva, in love with your Guru (spiritual teacher), in love with your fellow sevites, in love with the people who come to the center, and in love with the people who do not come to the center."

— Yoga Sutra

FEAR INTENTIONS

Courage is facing your fears and watching them back away.

— Yoga Sutra

If you can face your fear, you will go beyond it. Then you will become completely fearless. If you hold yourself back because of fear, you will lose everything.

— Yoga Sutra

Move, but don't move the way fear makes you move.

— Rumi

I will practice Acceptance of this moment as it is rather than as I think it should be. I will not struggle against the universe by struggling against this moment. My acceptance is total and complete...

I will take Responsibility for my situation and all things I see as problems, not blaming anyone or anything for the circumstances, including myself. I know that every problem is an opportunity in disguise, and this alertness to opportunities allows me to take this moment and transform it into a greater benefit...

Today my awareness will remain established in Defenselessness. I will relinquish the need to defend my point of view. I will feel no need to convince or persuade others to accept my point of view. I will remain open to all points of view and not be rigidly attached to any one of them.

— Deepak Chopra

Nothing real can be threatened. Nothing unreal exists. Herein lies the peace of God.

— A Course in Miracles

Move outside the tangle of fear-thinking. Live in silence.

— Rumi

Security is a superstition. It does not exist in Nature.

— Helen Keller

Forgiveness ends all suffering and loss.

Throughout the day, whenever I'm tempted to be fearful, I remind myself I can choose to experience Love instead.

I want to experience peace of mind right now. I happily let go of all attack thoughts and choose peace instead.

— Gerald Jampolsky

There is no greater illusion than fear,

no greater wrong than preparing to defend yourself,

no greater misfortune than having an enemy.

Whoever can see through all fear

will always be safe.

— Tao Te Ching

When I despair, I remember that all through history the way of truth and love has always won. There have been tyrants and murderers, and for a time, they can seem invincible, but in the end, they always fall. Think of it—always.

— Mahatma Gandhi

Whatever you fight, you strengthen, and what you resist, persists.

— Eckhart Tolle

Love dissolves Fear. May I always have the courage to lovingly respond to every situation, no matter how fearful.

— Lester Strong

Being mindful of fear allows it to become your teacher and gives purpose to what is otherwise meaningless suffering.

— Buddhist Teaching

Vulnerability is uncertainty, risk, and emotional exposure. Courage requires acting in the midst of uncertainty, risk, and emotional exposure. Hence there is no vulnera-bility without courage.

— Brené Brown

Either you do vulnerability or vulnerability does you.

It's so much easier to cause pain than to feel pain. Stop working your shit out on other people. Take individual responsibility for it.

— Brené Brown

Can't go it alone. We're hardwired for human connection. In the midst of loving and relationships, there is always suffering.

— Brené Brown

Only share with people who have earned the right to see your vulnerability. Your story is a privilege to hear, so only share it with people who deserve to hear it. Vulnerability minus boundaries is not vulnerability.

— Brené Brown

You don't measure vulnerability by the amount of disclo-sure you make. You measure it by the amount of courage it takes to show up and be seen when you can't control the outcome.

— Brené Brown

PURPOSE INTENTIONS

The purpose of life is undoubtedly to know oneself. We cannot do it unless we learn to identify ourselves with all that lives. The sum-total of that life is God.

— Gandhi

The best way to find yourself is to lose yourself in the service of others.

— Gandhi

Be the change you want to see in the world.

— Gandhi

To live simply is to live gently,

Keeping in mind always the needs

Of the planet, other creatures, and

The generations to come. In doing this

We lose nothing, because the interests

Of the whole naturally include our own.

— Eknath Easwaran

Never continue in a job you don't enjoy. If you're happy in what you're doing, you'll like yourself, you'll have inner peace. And if you have that, along with physical health, you will have had more success than you could possibly have imagined.

— Johnny Carson

You don't have to wait for something "meaningful" to come into your life so that you can finally enjoy what you do. There is more meaning in joy than you will ever need. The "waiting to start living" syndrome is one of the most common delusions of the unconscious state.

— Eckhart Tolle

If a man is called to be a street sweeper, he should sweep streets even as Michelangelo painted, or Beethoven composed music, or Shakespeare wrote poetry. He should sweep streets so well that all the hosts of heaven and earth will pause to say, "Here lived a great street sweeper who did his job well."

— Martin Luther King, Jr.

I am not sure exactly what heaven will be like, but I know that when we die and it comes time for God to judge us, he will not ask, "How many good things have you done in your life?" Rather, he will ask, "How much love did you put into what you did?"

— Mother Teresa

Don't ask what the world needs. Ask what makes you come alive and go do it. Because what the world needs is people who have come alive.

— Howard Thurman

The price of inaction is far greater than the cost of making a mistake. Do exactly what you would do if you felt most secure.

— Meister Eckhart

We begin to find and become ourselves when we notice how we are already found, already truly, entirely, wildly, and messily, marvelously who we were meant to be.

— Anne Lamott

If you prepare yourself at every point as well as you can... you will be able to grasp the opportunity for broader experience when it appears.

— Eleanor Roosevelt

Follow your bliss.

— Joseph Campbell

Work is love made visible. And when you work with love, you bind yourself to yourself and to one another and to God.

— Khalil Gibran

There is no greater gift you can give or receive than to honor your calling. It is why you were born. And how you become most truly alive.

— Oprah Winfrey

We are charged with the accountability of that which wishes to pass through us.

— Carl Jung

What a tragedy to spend our lives climbing the ladder of success only to find that it's leaning against the wrong wall.

— Marc Freedman

DEATH INTENTIONS

Never the Spirit was born—

The Spirit will cease to be, never.

Never was a time it was not—

End and beginning are dreams.

Birthless and deathless and changeless,

Abideth the Spirit forever.

Death doth not touch it at all.

— The Bhagavad Gita

We live in illusion, the appearance of things.

But there is a reality. We are that reality.

When you understand this, you see that you are nothing,

And being nothing, you are everything. That is all.

— Kalu Rinpoche

Death is nothing more than a migration of the soul

From this place to another.

— Plato

Do you see, oh my brothers and sisters, it is not

Chaos and death. It is form and union and plan.

It is eternal life. It is happiness.

— Emerson

Dear friend, please know as you pass by,

As you are now, so once was I.

As I am now, so you will be.

Prepare yourself to follow me.

— New England Gravestone

Death is our greatest challenge as well as our greatest spiritual opportunity.

By cultivating mindfulness, we can prepare ourselves for this final passage

By allowing nature, rather than Ego, to guide us.

In so doing, we become teachers to others and our best friends,

Looking beyond the body's death to the next stage of the Soul's adventure.

— Ram Dass

The Master gives herself up

To whatever the moment brings.

She knows that she is going to die,

And she has nothing left to hold on to:

No illusions in her mind,

No resistances in her body.

She doesn't think about her actions;

They flow from the core of her being.

She holds nothing back from life;

Therefore she is ready for death,

As one is ready for sleep

After a good day's work...

— Tao Te Ching

Death has nothing to do with

Going away.

The sun sets.

The moon sets.

But they are not gone...

— Rumi

If you realize that all things change,

There is nothing you will try to hold on to.

If you aren't afraid of dying,

There is nothing you can't achieve...

— Tao Te Ching

Life has no opposite. The opposite of death is birth. Life is eternal.

— Eckhart Tolle

Death is a stripping away of all that is not you.

The secret of life is to "die before you die"—

And find that there is no death.

— Eckhart Tolle

Though the ordinary human being looks upon death with dread and sadness, those who have gone before know it as a wondrous experience of peace and freedom. At death, you forget all the limitations of the physical body and realize how free you are.

For the first few seconds, there is a sense of fear—fear of the unknown, of something unfamiliar. But after that comes a great realization, a joyous sense of relief and freedom. You know that you exist apart from the mortal body.

Every one of us is going to die someday, so there is no use in being afraid of death. There is nothing to fear.

When death comes, laugh at it.

Our real Self is immortal. We may sleep for a little

while in that change called death, but we can never be destroyed. We exist, and that existence is eternal.

The wave comes to the shore and then goes back to the sea; it is not lost. It becomes one with the ocean, or returns again in the form of another wave.

This body has come, and it will vanish; but the essence within it will never cease to exist. Nothing can terminate that eternal Consciousness.

Even a particle of matter or a wave of energy is indestructible, as science has proved; the spiritual essence is also indestructible.

Matter undergoes change; the soul undergoes changing experiences. Radical changes are termed death, but death or a change in form does not change or destroy the spiritual essence.

The body is only a garment. How many times you have changed your clothing in this life, yet because of this, you would not say that you have changed. Similarly, when you give up this bodily dress at death, you do not change. You are just the same.

The word 'death' is a great misnomer, for there is no death.

— Paramahansa Yogananda

Appendix B - Hyperlinks

For easy access to all of the hyperlinks in this book, go to thegreatlifehandbook.com.

1. *Roots*
https://www.nytimes.com/2021/10/21/books/review/roots-alex-hale.html
2. UBUNTU
https://www.youtube.com/watch?v=44xbZ8MN1uk
3. Thich Nath Hanh on the Science of Meditation
https://www.youtube.com/shorts/uw1TJ87jGAQ
4. Unified Field Theory
https://en.wikipedia.org/wiki/Unified_field_theory
5. Implicate & Explicit Order
https://en.wikipedia.org/wiki/David_Bohm
6. *"I think therefore I am"*
https://1000wordphilosophy.com/2018/11/26/descartes-i-think-therefore-i-am/
7. *"I am aware of my thoughts, therefore I am."*
https://researchfeatures.com/sartres-idea-of-consciousness-ego-brief-
    sketch/#:~:text=The%20ego%2C%20according%20to%20Sartre,ele-
    ment%20of%20the%20human%20entity.
8. Tat Tvam Asi
https://www.thehindu.com/society/faith/tat-tvam-asi-explained/arti
    cle36701998.ece
9. chin mudra
https://www.tummee.com/yoga-poses/chin-mudra
10. *Stillness Speaks*
https://www.shortform.com/summary/stillness-speaks-summary-eckhart-
    tolle?utm_source=google&utm_medium=cpc&gad_source=1&gclid=
    CjwKCAiAjKu6BhAMEiwAx4UsAgc_xDwfVueZziyVqx3VxebHfisiwIcv3-
    77EzJt9p6HPe4X_DEychoCow8QAvD_BwE
11. *Bhagavad Gita*
https://www.shortform.com/summary/the-bhagavad-gita-vb13747-f-summary-
    eknath-easwaran?utm_source=google&utm_medium=cpc&gad_source=1&
    gclid=Cj0KCQiA6Ou5BhCrARIsAPoTxrBFRnlkUct30u88n-XQ9Xqt6Af5p
    HX2GJ3Gkl_te7GvHYDwvu1-RlQaAjiZEALw_wcB

12. *How We Live is How We Die*

*https://www.shambhala.com/how-we-live-is-how-we-die.html?srsltid=
AfmBOopiim_4Mk7JoxFl6f9emrRlEhZuaV3Lfjf49kVYwXd8uQ8AkF30*

13. *HamSa*

https://yinyoga.com/yinsights/hamsa-mantra/

14. *Chakra Tune-up With Himalayan Bowls*

https://www.youtube.com/watch?v=-ar9vsmFhJU&t=7s

15. Redwood Tingsha Meditation

*https://www.google.com/search?q=redwood+tingsha+meditation&rlz=
1C5MACD_enUS1038US1038&oq=redwood+tingsha+meditation&gs_l
crp=EgZjaHJvbWUyBggAEEUYOTIGCAEQRRhAMgYIAhBFGDwyBgg
DEEUYPTIGCAQQRRg90gEJMTY1NTBqMGo0qAIAsAIA&sourceid=
chrome&ie=UTF-8#fpstate=ive&vhid=gHvzAs1IDUOycM&vld=cid:
f1a3a3cc,vid:I3zJJR-uHeI,st:0&vssid=global.*

16. *Chakras*

https://www.healthline.com/health/fitness-exercise/7-chakras#Chakra-101

17. Eckhart Tolle Meditation Practice

https://www.youtube.com/watch?v=S2GjkQxtpF4

18. *Larisa Halilović on Finding your Values*

https://www.youtube.com/watch?v=mL4l75rMIiQ&t=33s

9. Personal Values List - Break the Twitch

https://www.breakthetwitch.com/values/

20. Sample online journal

*https://penzu.com/?gad_source=1&gclid=CjwKCAjwg-24BhB_EiwA1ZOx8gUI
Ws5FTA-gY5lXe7Xumga3NwZ3jqUEY_ZOuZEkFJXsEcMMJTbV5Bo
Cpr4QAvD_BwE*

21. *Maya*

https://www.ananda.org/yogapedia/maya/

22. *Scent of a Woman*

https://www.youtube.com/watch?v=hHtFAd8yt2o

23. *Tibetan Book of the Dead*

*https://kadampa-center.org/sites/default/files/The%20Tibetan%20Book%20of%
20the%20Dead%20First%20Complete%20Translation%20%28Penguin%
20Classics%20Deluxe%20Edition%29.pdf*

24. *The Four Agreements*

https://www.scribd.com/document/683065309/The-four-Agreements

25. *The Seven Spiritual Laws of Success*

https://www.scribd.com/document/229938526/7-Spiritual-Laws-of-Success

26. *Positive Psychology*

https://www.psychologytoday.com/us/basics/positive-psychology

27. Esther Perel

https://www.youtube.com/watch?v=ObtmLBOfIRM&t=123s

28. Leonard Cohen singing *Hallelujah*

https://www.youtube.com/watch?v=YrLk4vdY28Q

29. Leonard Cohen PBS Interview

https://www.youtube.com/watch?v=8KzSoUd76qo&t=7s

30. *wabi sabi*

https://www.youtube.com/watch?v=8mtvCJPoYrk

31. *Loving What is*

https://www.youtube.com/watch?v=BiaCfVoWUbo